During My Time

Florence Davidson, 1980

During My Time

FLORENCE EDENSHAW DAVIDSON, A HAIDA WOMAN

Margaret B. Blackman

University of Washington Press
Seattle and London

Douglas & McIntyre, Ltd.
Vancouver/Toronto

This book was published with the assistance of a grant from the National Endowment for the Humanities.

Library of Congress Cataloging-in-Publication Data

Blackman, Margaret B.
  During my time.

  Bibliography:p.
  Includes index.
  1. Davidson, Florence Edenshaw, 1896-
2. Haida Indians–Biography. 3. Haida Indians–Women.
4. Indians of North America–Northwest coast of North
America–Women. I. Davidson, Florence Edenshaw,
1896- . II. Title.
E99.H2D383   1982   970.004'97[B]   82–8674
ISBN 0-295-95943-6 (cl)   AACR2
ISBN 0-295-96219-4 (pbk)

Canadian Cataloging-in-Publication Data

Blackman, Margaret B. (Margaret Berlin), 1944-
  During my time

Includes index.
Bibliography:p
ISBN 0-88894-351-2 (bound). —ISBN
  0-88894-400-4 (pbk.)
1. Davidson, Florence Edenshaw, 1986-
2. Haida Indians–Biography. 3. Haida
Indians–Women. 4. Indians of North America–
Northwest Coast of North America–Women.
I. Davidson, Florence Edenshaw, 1896-
II. Title
E99.H2D383   1982   970.004'97   C84-4440-2

Frontispiece photograph of Florence Davidson by Margaret Blackman

For her children, their spouses,
and all who know her as "Nani"

PREFACE

Poets and photographers refer to them as the Misty Isles—the Queen Charlottes, nestled in the sometimes turbulent waters off the northern mainland coast of British Columbia. These islands hold for me, as for the many others who live or visit here, a special enchantment. I have marked my life's most weighty problems in measured footsteps along the sandy miles of spruce-rimmed North Beach, watched the moon rise in full splendor above the yawning tranquil mouth of the Yakoun River where the Masset Haida go to fish each spring for salmon. And, at times, my mind has glimpsed fleeting shadows from the islands' past: Haida hunters in search of seals at the land's edge, women and children roasting the lupine roots they called "black bear's tail" in stone-lined pits on the meadowland of Rose Spit. For me, there stand before the mile-long row of modern houses in the Haida village of Masset fading images of cedar-plank community houses, oversize animals entwined in their skyward climb up cedar totem poles, and long, graceful canoes beached above the high-tide mark, images known now only in photographs taken by adventurous visitors from the last century. As late as 1970, when I first came to know the Queen Charlottes, these images were recalled in the memories of a few elderly Haida who had been born in the old-style houses, but today, eleven years later, they and their remembrances have gone to their ancestors.

I have made the journey from the urban East to the Queen Charlottes several times. In 1970 I came with my former husband, Jim Blackman, to spend the year studying Haida culture history gleaned from the memories of Haida elders and from the volumes of museum and archival photographs I had amassed. Two years passed before I returned to the islands in the summer of 1973 to research changing Haida kinship organization. The following summer I came again, to study the traditional and changing relationship of the Haida people to their natural environment. In August of 1975 I flew to the Charlottes with my colleague and friend, now husband, Ed Hall to introduce him to "my" Misty Isles.

In 1977 I made the journey twice, ostensibly for study purposes but as much for sentimental as academic reasons. I had come to fulfill a promise made to Florence Edenshaw Davidson of Masset in 1973: we would, one of these days, sit together and record her life history, which would eventually be published as a book. I had never seriously questioned why I would do it, save when justification had to be made to secure funding for the project. Justification for me lay in my personal relationship to Florence Davidson. She had served as my main female teacher in my previous Haida studies and we had developed a close working relationship; she had taken me into her home and I lived with her during most of my field research; but, most importantly, she accepted me, as she has others, as a grandchild. To live once again in her home, to learn from her, to be a recipient of her sparkling humor and grandmotherly love—these were the main reasons I found myself on a plane from Vancouver bound for the Queen Charlotte Islands in January and again in June of 1977.

Then as I flew northward, and now as I write, my visual images of Florence Davidson are vivid. A short, sturdy woman whose once black hair has grayed in front, she has a dignity and bearing which make her seem taller than she really is. In 1977 she was eighty-one, but her physical strength and energy, her involvement in Masset ceremonial life, and her mental spirit belie her years. I see her now, dressed in an elegant long black dress, Haida carved gold bracelets encircling both arms, standing to make a speech in Haida at a feast, most likely a feast she herself has hosted. In the early mornings I often awoke to find her in a housedress or bathrobe pummelling down the mound of bread dough rising in an enormous enamel washbasin on the kitchen table. I remember her from 1973 in slacks, headscarf, and gumboots, expertly slicing salmon at her Yakoun River fish camp where I had joined her for the several days she spent putting up her annual stock of sockeye. I recall a photograph I took of her in 1971, dressed in hat and gloves about to depart for an Anglican Church Women's conference at a Nass River Indian village. Her gloved hands clutched two large tins of seaweed which she had dried to trade with the Nass natives for eulachon grease. Most often, though, I see her laughing, talking in Haida to a visitor over a cup of tea as they sit at the old oak table in her ample kitchen.

I have seen her, too, through the eyes of others. Weaving a hat, she smiles from the pages of Ulli Steltzer's *Indian Artists at Work* (1976). She appears in two National Film Board of Canada films ("Haida Carver" and "This was the Time"), which feature her artist grandson Robert Davidson; and not long ago in a CBC television advertisement for Canadian Indian art, she was sewing a button blanket at her dining room table. Her charm infects even those who do not know her as I do. The two work-study students at the college where I teach became fascinated with the personality on the tapes they were laboriously transcribing. "Such a neat lady. What a sense of humor," they exclaimed. And, at their request, I brought out slides and photographs so they might better visualize the woman whose voice they had come to know.

Florence Davidson has served as a willing informant for several researchers besides myself, on projects ranging from ethnobotany to linguistics to native education. Though a meticulous chronicler of her own culture, it is neither the intellectual challenge nor the documentary significance of her role that motivates her; rather, she dwells on the people behind the projects. "I think of them just like my own," she says of most of them. Virtually all younger people who pass through her large home as boarders and/or researchers are soon instructed to call her "Nani" (Haida for "grandmother"). She once laughingly remarked, "Everybody calls me Nani. I must be the world's nani." The universal grandmother: indulgent but teasing, somewhat aghast at the strange doings of the modern generation yet still eager to try new things, knowledgeable in the old ways, retrospective. That is how I have come to know her as Nani; that is how I hope readers of this work will see her.

Margaret B. Blackman
July 1981

ACKNOWLEDGMENTS

Many people have contributed in various ways to this manuscript, and to them I extend my heartfelt thanks.

Marjorie Mitchell gave me a summer home in Victoria where most of the writing of this manuscript took place. She and Anna Franklin offered invaluable support and advice during the writing, provided photographs, and shared in Nani's world with me. Barbara Efrat of Victoria provided housing during my archival research in the summer of 1978 and supplied me with cassette tapes through the Linguistics Division of the British Columbia Provincial Museum.

Susan Kenyon critically read the manuscript and offered extensive commentary. I have also benefited from the comments and suggestions of Betty Berlin, Barbara Hall, Edwin S. Hall, Jr., Robert Davidson, Dorothy Grant, Miles Richardson, and Ulli Steltzer, who read the manuscript or portions of it. Julie Kokis, Tina Howe, and Elizabeth Quinlan transcribed the forty-five hours of life-history tapes. Mary Beth Johnson and Debora Lang typed the manuscript. Norm Frisch prepared the map and genealogy. Robert Levine and Barbara Efrat offered assistance with the orthography.

Research was funded by an Urgent Ethnology contract from the National Museums of Canada, a National Endowment for the Humanities Summer Research Fellowship, and a grant from the Phillips Fund of the American Philosophical Society.

Many people from the Queen Charlottes have contributed to my research. Lola Dixon first introduced me to Florence Davidson in 1970; Howard Phillips lent photographs for inclusion in the manuscript; Dixie and Howard Post provided hospitality and friendship during the seasons of my field research. Nani's nine children and their spouses (Alfred and Rose Davidson, Virginia and Dave Hunter, Claude and Vivian Davidson, Sarah Davidson, Primrose and Victor Adams, Emily and Dave Goertzen, Myrtle and Sid Kerrigan, Aggie and Sam Davis, Merle and Knud Andersen, Clara and Brian Hugo) have provided many kindnesses during the years of my comings and goings to the Queen Charlottes. Others from Haida Masset, some now deceased, have shaped my image of the islands, and I acknowledge in particular the assistance of William and Flora Russ, June and Reno Russ, Percy Brown, Amanda Edgars, William and Emma Matthews, and Peter Hill. I am grateful to Nani's grandson Robert for the use of his dogfish design in chapters 4–9.

More than anyone else, Florence Davidson has given substance to my image of the Queen Charlotte Islands and their people. As teacher, friend, and grandmother she has enriched my life, and I thank her for sharing her life history with me and with readers of this book.

Royalties accruing to the author from publication of this book will go to Florence Davidson.

ORTHOGRAPHY

Haida words are spelled phonetically throughout the text. Although there are several works on the Haida language (see Levine 1973 and Lawrence 1977 for works written for a general audience), there is no standard orthography for Haida. Vowels and consonants not listed are pronounced the same as their English equivalents. Haida place names are Anglicized to conform to current map usage.

a	as in f<u>a</u>ther
ae	as in <u>a</u>t
E	as in l<u>e</u>t
e	as in l<u>a</u>te
i	as in b<u>ee</u>t
ɨ	as in <u>i</u>t
ə	as in <u>a</u>ccompany
ay	as in l<u>i</u>ght
u	as in t<u>u</u>ne
ʊ	as in p<u>u</u>t
o	as in <u>o</u>at
ł	unvoiced l, made by placing the tongue in the l position and blowing air out laterally
z	as in dog<u>s</u>
c	as in <u>ch</u>urch
x	as in the German *ich* ("I")
q	made like k only farther back in the throat
ʔ	glottal stop; the sound or "pause" that occurs in "oh oh"
'	all sounds followed by an apostrophe are made with a constricted glottis
ʕ	a sound produced by constriction of the pharyngeal cavity; similar to the sound one makes when blowing on eyeglasses prior to cleaning them

Contents

ILLUSTRATIONS

During My Time

CHAPTER 1

The Life-History Project

. . . the life history is still the most cognitively rich and humanly understandable way of getting at an inner view of culture. [No other type of study] can equal the life history in demonstrating what the native himself considers to be important in his own experience and how he thinks and feels about that experience. [Phillips 1973:201]

THE LIFE HISTORY IN ANTHROPOLOGY

The writing of native life histories has long been regarded by anthropologists as a legitimate as well as popular approach to understanding and describing other cultures.[1] In 1922, for example, anthropologist Elsie Clews Parsons wrote in the preface to her biography of a Zuni woman: "In our own complex culture biography may be a clarifying form of description. Might it not avail at Zuni?" (Parsons 1922:158). Alfred Kroeber, who wrote the introduction to *American Indian Life*, in which Parsons' article appears, believed that the unique contribution of this collection of biographical sketches was their insight into the social psychology of the American Indian. Unfortunately, most of the contributors to this volume found it necessary to fictionalize the life histories, inventing characters for the ethnographic data on the individual life cycle.

1. *Lives: An Anthropological Approach to Biography*, which appeared just as this book was going to press, provides an introduction "to the full historical and conceptual development of the life-history method in anthropology . . . and discusses the relevance of this method to a wider audience" (Langness and Frank 1981:5).

3

While it is fortunate that fictionalized life histories have been the exception in anthropological research, their very existence points to the significance of the medium for presenting the cultural record. The utility and success of the life-history approach in anthropology can be attributed to a number of factors. In the first place, the basic fabric of ethnology is woven from the scraps of individuals' lives, from the experiences and knowledge of individual informants. Many ethnographic accounts of subsistence activities, marriage, and ritual observances, for example, are derived directly from the personal experiences of members of a culture, and as anthropologists work closely with selected informants, the presentation of ethnographic data from the longitudinal perspective of the individual life is not surprising. "Culture" as lived by the individual represents the ultimate inside view, and the life history thus serves as a useful complement to the standard ethnography.

The life history also complements the ethnographic account by adding to the descriptive an affective or experiential dimension. We know, for example, from early ethnographic accounts of Haida culture the form and function of the girl's puberty ritual and the structure of Haida marriage, and from more recent ethnohistoric studies we know the changes wrought in Haida culture following contact. But these sources do not really address the question of meaning: What was the puberty seclusion really like? What did it mean to the individual to have his or her marriage arranged at an early age? How did individuals respond to various cultural changes? The life history is uniquely suited to addressing this kind of question.

The life history is also an appropriate medium for the study of acculturation. In many cultures the lives of natives span periods of critical and rapid culture change; the life history affords a personalized, longitudinal view of these changes.

Kluckhohn (1945), in a now classic article on the use of personal documents in anthropology, adds that life histories can be avenues to understanding status and role, individual variation within cultural patterns of behavior, personality structure, deviance, and idiosyncratic variation.

Native Americans have been by far the most popular subject material for life histories. Interest in the lives of American Indians began in the nineteenth century as famous and notorious Indian leaders commanded the attention of the public and sparked the writing of romantic and sentimental biographies. Langness (1965), for example, lists thirty-six American Indian life histories published between 1825 and 1900. A more recent and comprehensive accounting of Native American life histories (Brumble 1981), which brings the list up to the 1980s, contains over five hundred entries. Were one to include the numerous non-first-person accounts of Native American lives, which Brumble does not, this total would be considerably larger. The earliest anthropological life histories were also of American Indians (Kroeber 1908; Radin 1913). The recently published biographical sketches in *American Indian Intellectuals* (Liberty 1978) point to a still-current interest in the "great men"[2] of native society, though simultaneously there has been a growing interest in recording the lives of ordinary Native Americans.

Inspired in part by Franz Boas' early interest in the individual and his field research on the Northwest Coast, a number of life histories of Northwest Coast natives have been published over the years.[3] Edward Sapir included a fictionalized life history of a Nootka trader in *American Indian Life* (Parsons 1922); Diamond Jenness (1955) relied upon the personal reminiscences of "Old Pierre" to compile his treatise on Katzie supernatural beliefs; and Marius Barbeau's discussion of Haida argillite carvings (1957) included data on the artistic careers of the major Haida slate carvers. Further recognition of the importance of genealogical and life-history data to the study of native Indian art in British Columbia led the Vancouver Centennial Museum in 1977 to initiate a comprehensive collection of biographical data on British Columbia's Indian artists.

Two Northwest Coast life-history documents span successive generations of recent Southern Kwakiutl culture history and are particularly valuable for their documentation of continuity and change in that culture. In 1940 Kwakiutl Chief Charlie Nowell dictated his life story to Clellan Ford (1941), and in the 1960s James Sewid related his personal history, with the editorial assistance of anthropologist James Spradley (1969). Aside from Barbeau's brief biographical sketches in *Haida Carvers in Argillite* (1957) and the account of Chief Gəniyá ("Cunneah") in Robinson's *Sea Otter Chiefs* (1978), the only Haida life history is that of Peter Kelly of Skidegate (Morley 1967). To date, no life histories of native Northwest Coast women have been published, though as early as 1930 several short life histories of Kwakiutl women were collected by Julia Averkieva, a student of Boas (Rohner 1966:198).

2. Two of the biographies included there are of women: Sarah Winnemucca (Northern Paiute) by Catherine Fowler and Flora Zuni (Zuni) by Triloki Nath Panday.

3. Boas (1943) later eschewed the life history as a legitimate approach to the study of culture.

In fact, for native North America as a whole there are more than three times the number of male life histories as female life histories. At least in the case of the life histories authored or collected by anthropologists, this imbalance is in large part due to the fact that male ethnographers, who until recently have greatly outnumbered female ethnographers, understandably came to know and work more closely with the male members of the cultures they studied. Then, too, as Rosaldo (1974) has noted, men live much of their lives in the public arena, as policy makers, warriors, intellectuals, and philosophers in native societies. Given such roles it is not surprising that anthropologists should have found the lives of men more visible, interesting, absorbing, and significant than the lives of women. This viewpoint has often affected even those who do write about native women's lives. Ruth Underhill, for example, justifies Papago Maria Chona's narrative by demonstrating her affiliation with important men: "As a woman she could take no active part in the ceremonial life. But her father was a governor and a warrior; her brother and husband were shamans; her second husband was a song leader and composer" (Underhill 1936:4). She does add, however, that a Papago woman's life is interesting in and of itself "because in this culture, there persists strongly the fear of woman's impurity with all its consequent social adjustments."

I suspect that anthropologists are more influenced by their own cultural background than they would like to acknowledge. Perhaps the relative neglect of women's lives in other cultures stems also from the fact that autobiography in the Western tradition has been primarily a male form. As Pomerleau notes:

> The traditional view of women is antithetical to the crucial motive of autobiography—a desire to synthesize, to see one's life as an organic whole, to look back for a pattern. Women's lives are fragmented. . . . the process is not one of growth, of evolution; rather . . . earlier and more decisively than for a man, the curve of a woman's life is seen by herself and society to be one of deterioration and degeneration. Men may mature, but women age. [1980:37]

In the same volume Jelinek summarizes, "Insignificance, indeed, expresses the predominant attitude of most [literary] critics towards women's lives" (Jelinek 1980:4).

Only recently have anthropologists taken the view that, even in the absence of criteria such as a belief in woman's impurity or relationships to powerful men, women's lives are inherently worthy of consideration. If we are to understand women and their roles in cross-cultural perspective, it is axiomatic that we know the breadth and depth of their life experiences, the ordinary as well as the extraordinary. Margaret Mead has provided us with the latter type of document in her autobiography *Blackberry Winter* (1972), and in the wake of the women's movement a number of anthropological monographs that focus on the lives of ordinary women have been published (e.g., Strathern 1972; Jones and Jones 1976; Weiner 1976; Dougherty 1978; Kelley 1978). Accounts of native women's lives written for a more general audience have also appeared in recent years. In the native North American literature are an overview of the female life cycle in many different tribes (Neithammer 1977), a biography of a well-known Ojibwa woman (Vanderburgh 1977), and autobiographies written by a part-Cree woman (Willis 1973) and a métis woman (Campbell 1973).

Florence Davidson's life history is the account of one who faithfully fulfilled the expected role of women in her society. For most of her life she has remained outside the public domain; above all else she has participated in her culture as mother and wife, and today she would undoubtedly sum up her identity in the word "Nani." Despite the social position she has enjoyed as the daughter of high-ranking parents and the esteem that she has earned, Florence Davidson views her life as "ordinary," in the sense of being uneventful. Once during our taping she sighed and then laughed, "If only I lied, it could be so interesting!" Aside from recounting the life experiences of an octogenarian Haida woman, her narrative presents a picture of an individual operating in a culture neither traditionally Haida nor fully Canadian, a culture undergoing tremendous change, yet intelligible and meaningful to one living in it.

The Haida had been exposed to Christianity for only about twenty years when Florence Davidson was born in 1896, and just fifteen years prior to her birth the Masset Haida had become reserve Indians. A few Haida were still living in cedar-plank houses when she was born. The female puberty seclusion was still practiced during her adolescence, and marriages were, as a rule, arranged. Her life spans the beginning and end of a resident Indian Agency in Masset, the development of schooling from the one-room mission school through the residential boarding schools to the modern public educational system, and the evolution of transportation from the dugout canoe to daily jet service on the Queen Charlotte Islands.

Florence remembers a time when the ceremonial button blankets, devised probably in the 1850s by native people, were disdained and her grandmother cut the small buttons from hers to give to her

granddaughters for their babies' clothes. Today Florence Davidson
has become perhaps the foremost Haida button blanket maker,
sewing exquisite appliquéd blankets from her grandson Robert's
patterns. She recalls the time in 1932 when William Matthews took
his uncle's place as town chief of Masset without a semblance of a
traditional installation ceremony. Forty-four years later when Oliver
Adams succeeded his uncle, William Matthews, he hired Florence
Davidson to cook for the feast; she sang a Haida song in his honor
and was recognized for her efforts at the potlatch marking his
chieftaincy.

There were no totem poles carved during Florence's childhood,
save the few commissioned of the last of the old carvers at five
dollars per foot by museum collectors. In 1969 Florence and Robert
Davidson gave a potlatch honoring the erection of the pole their
grandson Robert had carved for the Masset people. In short,
Florence Davidson's life weaves through a significant period of
Haida culture history, a time that saw the disappearance of many
traditional practices (the puberty ceremony, arranged marriages,
most forms of potlatching) and the rebirth of others (such as the
visual and performing arts).

RECORDING THE LIFE HISTORY

My only special preparations for the journey to Masset in January of
1977 included packing a wool shirt and rain slicker, a tape recorder
and forty hours of tape, a journal, a copy of Murdock's *Our Primitive
Contemporaries*, which contains a chapter on the Haida, and Clellan
Ford's life history of Charlie Nowell to show to Florence Davidson as
an example. I had not given extensive thought as to how we would
proceed, confident that the problem would resolve itself once I
arrived in Masset. My only worry was that I might have the same
experience as anthropologist Nancy Lurie, who secured in her first
brief session with Mountain Wolf Woman, the Winnebago woman's
entire life history (Lurie 1961:XIV). Luckily I need not have worried:
"I'm full of stories yet," Nani pronounced about halfway through
the project.

The quickest method of getting to Masset is to take a jet from
Vancouver to Prince Rupert and from there a float or amphibious
plane to New Masset on the islands. No matter how rough the
weather, I never fail to enjoy the forty-five minutes from Prince
Rupert to Masset. Ten minutes in the air, from a point not far out to
sea, one can see in the distance the long dark tongue of Rose Spit
licking the waters of Dixon Entrance. Minutes pass; the sand bluffs

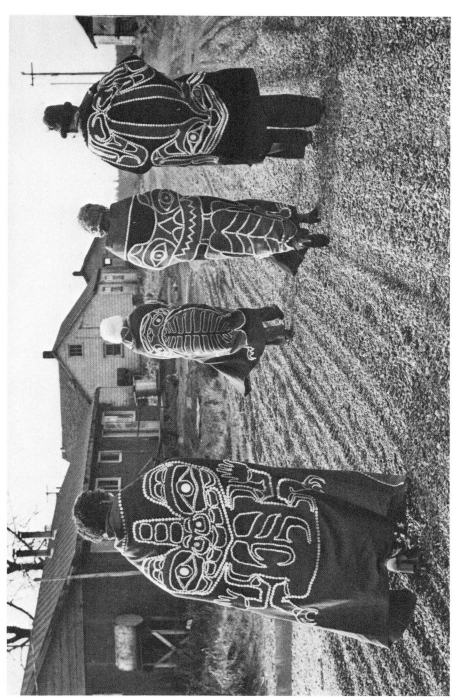

Button blankets worn by Florence Davidson (*left*) and other Masset Haida (photograph by Ulli Steltzer)

of the east coast of Graham Island make their appearance and the familiar landmark of Tow Hill rises several hundred feet into the air from the sands of North Beach. Geologists call Tow a volcanic intrusion; the Haida say he has a brother up Masset Inlet with whom he quarreled and that is why he stands alone now at the eastern extremity of the islands.

The plane flies over the ancient beach ridges ancestral to the present sands of North Beach and along Tow's backside. Yakin Point, where Tow paused in his westward migration, intrudes into the cold waters of Dixon Entrance, and beyond I recognize Kliki Creek where Nani, my anthropologist friend Marjorie Mitchell, and I went to collect spruce roots in the summer of 1974. We cross the mouth of Chowan Brook where Nani and her mother used to pick crabapples.

Ten miles from Masset is the "elephant pen," the local name for a Canadian Forces communications installation whose circular wires and fences look incongruous against the spruce and sand. The plane crosses the village of New Masset giving a glimpse of the Forces base and housing, the new hotel with the only beer parlor for miles around, the high school, the government wharf, the Co-op store. Water splashes the belly of the plane as it descends into the waters of Masset Inlet. Grudgingly, it struggles up on land coming to rest beside the tiny air terminal.

Haida Masset is three miles from New Masset and every taxi driver knows how to find Florence Davidson's house, or just about any other local house for that matter. Each time I return to the village, I mentally tick off the changes in its facade. Since I have been coming to the islands, the village has expanded as far southward toward New Masset as available reserve land will allow. It now moves westward, into the piled-up stumps of once timbered land. In January of 1977 traces of bright blue paint that adorned the exterior of Peter Hill's little house in 1970 had been washed away by the frequent rains, Alfred Davidson's fine large home had burned to the ground, Joe Weir's house had been razed to make way for a more modern one, the Yeltatzies had added a large picture window to the side of their home, and a rental duplex had been built catty-corner to Nani's house.

The taxi turns down an unpaved side street and comes to rest just short of the Anglican Church and Robert Davidson's magnificent totem pole. Despite the external changes in the village, Nani appears little different to me than she did in 1975 or in the years I knew her previous to that. She waits in the open door and enfolds me in a warm hug as I set down my suitcase.

Nani lives alone now in a sprawling one-story house, originally designed and built with the comforts of a large family in mind. Her front door opens into the spacious "front room," constructed as in other older Masset homes large enough to hold the entire adult population of the village. The front room has seen numerous feasts and potlatches, but normally it contains couches and overstuffed chairs pushed against its perimeter. The Sunday dining table sits in the room's center; plants fill the front window, and Robert Davidson's Haida designs, family photos, and religious mementos adorn the walls. Five bedrooms open off the large central room at its far end; at the opposite end, a leaded-glass door leads into the parlor—remodelled between January and June of 1977—panelled and carpeted in thick red plush. Many of our summer taping sessions were held in the quiet softness of this sitting room.

My favorite spot in the house and the room where I have spent the most time is Nani's expansive kitchen. I mark the passage of my Masset visits by the additions to her kitchen: new appliances, a new shelf, new flooring, a different color scheme. When I first came to Masset in 1970, the wash was done on the back porch in a wringer washer and Nani used to lug the heavy baskets of wet clothes across the yard to hang on the long clothesline, but by 1975 the old machine had been replaced by a new spin washer and dryer (gifts from a daughter and son-in-law), which occupy a prominent position in the kitchen. The village has had electricity since 1964 (and before, if one counts the portable generator that lighted the church and vicarage). Freezers and refrigerators followed in its wake, dramatically altering old patterns of food preservation and storage. Nani's kitchen contains both of these appliances, and a second freezer, filled to the top with venison, herring roe, berries, and fish, sits on the back porch pantry.

The most eye-catching feature of Nani's kitchen is the long bank of open shelves along one wall, which display some two hundred bone china cups and saucers, plus everyday dishes and the mugs from which we drink our breakfast coffee and afternoon tea. An oaken table, one of the few pieces salvaged from a house fire in 1952, faces the large kitchen window. In many ways this table is the focal point of the household. At it most meals are taken, visitors are received and served tea, and here Nani sits to rest from her baking or to weave a cedar bark hat. I have spent much of my fieldwork time here, too: interviewing Nani, writing in my journal at night, drinking coffee and gazing at the ever-moving waters of Masset Inlet, talking with Nani and others over tea.

By the summer of 1977, however, the view from the table had

Florence in her kitchen (photograph by Margaret Blackman)

changed. I recorded the change, somewhat petulantly, in my journal.

> I always liked sitting here and writing, looking up now and then to see Hannah (who lives next door) going in or out and collecting my thoughts as I watched the changing configurations of the western skies. But now a plank ledge runs the length of the window and the foliage of some fifty African violets sitting on it obscures much of the view. A fuchsia hangs from the ceiling and its embrace with a leggy geranium blots out Emma Matthews' house . . . ."

Even the long plank could not contain all the products of Nani's amazing green thumb; I discovered yet more African violets atop the washing machine, their leaves aflutter when the machine entered its spin cycle.

Nani's house is seldom inactive, and then only for a relatively short period, as she typically retires at 11:30 and arises as early as 5 A.M. Usually there are other boarders; various children, children-in-law, and grandchildren drop by during the day, and the health aide stops in on her rounds of the village. Hannah Parnell and Dora Brooks, Robert Davidson's lineage nieces, and Carrie Weir, a sister's daughter, appear every day or so to visit and have tea; and, not infrequently, someone from New Masset comes by to introduce a visiting friend to Nani.

Nani's tremendous energy is evident in the wonderful creative confusion that pervades her home. On a typical day loaves and loaves of bread rise in the kitchen under the protective covers of fresh linen towels; the combined vapors from a pot of stew and the kettle of "Indian medicine" beside it on the stove mingle and steam the kitchen window; an unfinished cedar bark hat stands spiderlike on the front room dining table; a small cat darts under a chair rustling the wide dry strips of cedar bark draped over it; Nani's crocheting lies where she left it on one of the front room chesterfields; the kitchen radio blaring messages to people in remote mainland communities competes with "The Edge of Night" emanating from the television in the front room; in the smokehouse adjacent to the house, Nani hangs halibut fillets on racks above the smoldering alder fire. Such was the setting in which Nani related her life story to me. Why she agreed to relate it is the result of several factors, among them her familiarity with anthropological inquiry, the compatibility of the life history mode with Haida values, and, not insignificantly, her relationship to me.

From the time she was very young Florence Davidson was aware of the interest of outsiders in Haida culture and artifacts. Her father worked for C. F. Newcombe of the Provincial Museum in Victoria as an informant and artist, and Florence recalls Newcombe's many visits to her father's home. She is too young to have had personal memories of John Swanton, who relied upon both her father and her uncle as informants and resided with the latter during his fieldwork in 1900–1901, but she may have heard them speak of him. In the later years of her marriage the Davidson home was frequented by the occasional anthropologist. Wilson Duff, for example, interviewed Florence more than once about her father and his forebears, and Mary Lee Stearns visited the Davidson home several times in 1965–66 to interview Robert Davidson during the course of her study of contemporary Masset culture (Stearns 1975, 1981).

Following the death of her husband in 1969, Florence emerged as a knowledgeable elder in her own right. In addition to her work with me, which began in 1970, she served as an informant on Haida ethnobotany for Nancy Turner in 1970 and 1971 (Turner 1974). In 1974 Florence was one of several Haida elders who contributed data to Marjorie Mitchell for a multi-media curriculum project on the Haida. In the early 1970s Florence worked briefly with linguists Barbara Efrat and Robert Levine of the British Columbia Provincial Museum, and since 1975 she has served as a linguistic informant for John Enrico, now a permanent boarder in her home. Moreover, she has appeared at museum openings as an elder ambassador of her culture, publicly demonstrated her skills at basket and button blanket making, and welcomed into her Masset home countless friends of white friends interested in Haida culture and eager to learn something of it from this grandmotherly representative.

In a brief life history of Flora Zuni, Panday cautions that the life history is not a natural or universal narrative mode among American Indians, noting that "Pueblo traditions do not provide any model of such confessional introspection" (1978:217). I am not certain if the life history is a Haida narrative form, but certainly as an anthropological form it is compatible with Haida traditions. The phrase used repeatedly by Florence Davidson during the course of her narration and selected by her as the title of this work—"during my time"—is a free translation of an often used Haida time referent, *di ʔeneng ge gut ʔn di unsiding*, "I see it [or, I know it] all of my lifetime." Such personalization of events goes hand-in-hand with the well-known emphasis in Northwest Coast culture upon the individual. The importance of rank, the feasting and potlatching that encouraged competition and individual expression, the custom of acquiring newly invented names at potlatches, and the mortuary potlatch as a vehicle for formally remembering a person long after his or her death (see Blackman 1973), all exemplify the significance of the individual in traditional Haida culture. Though Florence lamented the ordinariness of her life, the question "Why would anyone be interested in my life story?" understandably never arose.

Finally, although some anthropologists, such as Kluckhohn (1945:97), have regretted the intrusion of the anthropologist into the native life-history document, it goes without saying that the relationship between anthropologist and life-history subject is critical to the telling of the story in the first place and ultimately to the understanding of the final record. I agree with Brumble, who notes that "much of the fascination [with life histories is] a result of, rather than in spite of, their being so often collaborative" (1981:2).

Florence Davidson and I come from different worlds and different generations. Her children, the welfare of her family, and the church have been the focus of her long life; I have no children and at the center of my life is my academic career. She has lived the life of a housewife and mother, and I have not. How strange I must sometimes seem to her, spending long periods of time far from home, traveling freely, childless at an age when I should have a large family of my own. "How's your big family," she often teases me when we talk long distance. I once asked her what I might do to show I had "respect for myself," an important Haida virtue. "Dress up and stay home," she retorted, with laughter in her eyes. Yet our cultural, social, and age differences are softened by the mutual respect and affection we have developed over the years of our collaboration and friendship. My own grandmothers, strong, creative women and important figures in my childhood, did not survive into my adulthood. In many important ways, Nani has filled that gap in my life. Her life history was given to me, I think, as an anthropologist dedicated to learning the "old-fashioned ways," as a granddaughter curious about a grandmother's past, and as a woman interested in the events and people that shape women's lives. I doubt that Florence Davidson could have comfortably related her life history to me before I had established my commitment to learning about her culture, and I am certain that she could not have told her story to a man.

Although I had written Nani regarding arrangements for the project, we did not discuss it in any detail until my arrival in Masset. That first night I indicated to Nani that it would be nice to include what she knew about her ancestors. She thought for a moment and began relating how her father and grandfather had seen lucky signs in the woods, how her mother and her mother's mother's sister had been rescued from the smallpox epidemic, and how her grandfather had been called to take the chieftainship at Kiusta. When I protested that I had not yet unpacked my tape recorder, she replied, smiling, "It's OK, I was just practicing for tomorrow."

The following day she deliberated for some time about where to begin her narrative and settled on the drowning of her brother Robert, which occurred one month before her birth. From that point on, however, there was little chronological order to the narrative. Often she would select a topic to initiate the day's recording: "Let's talk about when my mother and I used to go for spruce roots"; or, "Did I tell you about the time when we built this house?" On other occasions she would leave the decision up to me, asking, "What shall we talk about?" or commanding, "You ask me questions." I would then pick a topic from the growing list I had compiled since my first day into the project.

When Nani was bereft of life-history memories we would explore kinship, reincarnation, Haida names, and numerous other ethnographic topics that I felt I had not sufficiently covered in my previous research. To a large extent my own interests biased the life-history data I obtained. For example, my concern with Haida ceremonial life, modern Masset's primary link with the past, led me to inquire repeatedly about feasts and potlatches given by ancestors and relatives. My interest in pollution taboos resulted in a lengthy digression into puberty and pregnancy proscriptions and male/female separation, topics that were not of as much interest to Nani. Because missionaries long ago had discouraged the custom and imposed European standards of decorum upon the Haida, Nani was somewhat embarrassed to discuss her puberty seclusion knowing that the account might be published. I, on the other hand, felt the subject significant enough to pursue until she had exhausted her memory. In addition, my view of life history as retrospective led me at certain times to ask questions that might elicit reflective responses. Typical examples include: What makes you happiest? When are the saddest times? What are the biggest changes you have seen? What would you most like to be remembered for? How would you describe yourself? Accordingly, Florence's "Reflections" (pp. 136–38) consist primarily of answers to questions that I posed.

Understandably, Nani sometimes dwelt on topics that were of great importance in her own life but not of as much interest to me as an anthropologist, in particular the impact of the church on her life, her role in it, and the meaning of Christianity to her. I do not know what form the life history might have taken had I avoided any intrusion, but given our relationship that would have been impossible. The final narrative is a measure both of our collaboration and of our sometimes divergent interests.

The schedule of our work was dictated by Nani's daily routine and the time constraints of my short field visits. We worked in the morning, the afternoon, sometimes after dinner, and occasionally just before bedtime. Most of the time we were alone, and when visitors called, our work was put aside. Often after a long day Nani lay on a chesterfield in the front room and I sat on the floor holding the microphone toward her. Sometimes, to avoid the noise and activity of the kitchen, we retired to her bedroom; she sat on her bed and leaned back against the wall, crocheting as she talked, except on Sundays when she put her handiwork aside. At times she wove on one of her cedar bark hats at the dining table. Once I taped her as she whittled cedar splits to be threaded through the black cod she was preparing to smoke. A song she sang on that occasion is punctuated by the sound of metal cutting red cedar. I sometimes joined her in activity. In January 1977, she gave a memorial feast in honor of her sister's daughter from Seattle who had died the preceding November, and we tried to tape in the kitchen amidst the preparations. Nani filled tarts with raspberry jam and I punched a plastic pattern into fourteen dozen doughy buns while we discussed earlier feasts. The quietest, most comfortable place to talk, though, proved to be the front parlor, where we worked during most of the June 1977 session.

Place or context played a considerable role in triggering Nani's memory. As we sat at the kitchen table one January day, the rain pelting the kitchen window reminded her of *q'ən dleł* ("everything's scarce"), the traditional Haida term for this time of year; a discussion of the seasons followed. Baking bread one Monday morning Nani recalled the days when she used to bake in the summertime at North Island for the fishermen. A juvenile eagle that scavenged a piece of drying halibut in June reminded Nani of her first attempt at slicing halibut and the chiding she received from her step-grandfather for the jagged-edged fillets she had hung to dry. Sometimes discussions of the project with other villagers brought to mind events from the past. Emma Matthews once reminded Nani of a play wedding they had staged as children. Some topics were easier for Nani to discuss than others. She recounted deaths in the family and the events leading to them in great detail, but when I asked her to describe the village and certain villagers as she remembered them from childhood, the details were sparse. I once asked her to describe her aunt, Martha Edenshaw; puzzling a moment over my request, she pointed to a photograph on the wall and answered, "She looks

Margaret Blackman and Florence Davidson, 1979 (photograph by Anna Franklin)

just like her picture." "But how do *you* think of her?" I continued. "I think of her just like the picture," Nani responded unhesitatingly.

Nani was aware of numerous gaps in her narrative. When I talked to her on the phone between my infrequent visits to Masset, she would often say, "after you left I remembered lots of things. I wish I could write them down because I forget them." Subsequent visits in 1978, 1979, 1980, and 1981 brought more reminiscences, but undoubtedly there are events and thoughts that she might wish to include which have eluded her memory. Occasionally, too, Nani was unable to remember something in the detail that I would have liked, reminding me quite appropriately, "It wasn't important to me then; how was I supposed to know that white people might be interested in it years later?"

From time to time, Nani's mischievous sense of humor crept into our work. Discussing her father's house where she had spent her childhood, I asked what it was like inside. She retorted that it was five stories, had "spring beds," and was covered in thick, thick carpeting. "I'm getting crazier than ever—what if you write that down," she said, dissolving in laughter. I recorded the contexts of all our taping sessions in the daily journal I kept, a practice I have always followed in fieldwork. Later, the journal became invaluable as I tried to remember what the house looked like that June, why Nani recalled this or that on a particular day, or why a certain subject had been sparingly discussed.

Florence Davidson's narrative is a circumspect one. Though she related to me both off and on tape things she did not wish to appear in print, her recollections by and large are devoid of the petty jealousies and rivalries that are part of the fabric of Masset life. There is little mention of the misdoings of self and others: illicit sexual liaisons (which figure prominently in some native male life histories[4]), witchcraft, or feuds between families. "I don't tell everything—what's no good," she said. Throughout our work Florence was conscious that the final product was to be a public document, though I imagine she was more concerned about its public status within her own community than in the larger world. This consciousness clearly guided not only what she related but how it was related. This bias may be characteristic of autobiography, regardless of culture. Jelinik, for example, speaking of autobiography in the Western tradition, notes:

> Irrespective of their professions or of their differing emphases in subject matter, neither women nor men are likely to explore or reveal painful and intimate memories in their autobiographies. . . . The admission of intense feelings of hate, love and fear, the disclosure of explicit sexual encounters, or the details of painful psychological experiences are matters on which autobiographers are generally silent. [1980:10, 12]

The division of the narrative into chapters is an artifact of my own thinking, not that of Florence Davidson's, although I did discuss its organization with her in the summer of 1978, and the chronology closely parallels the traditional life stages distinguished among the Haida. Nani requested that I edit the narrative to "fix it up" and "make it look right." I rearranged the narrative in chronological order, made certain grammatical and tense changes, and deleted redundancies, but those who know Nani will recognize her style of speaking. A section of the original narrative is presented in the appendix so readers may see its unedited form. Unfortunately, neither the original transcription nor the final edited version can adequately capture Florence Davidson's personality—the inflection

---

4. Charlie Nowell, for example, discusses his premarital and extramarital affairs (which he estimates at more than two hundred) quite openly and in some detail (Ford 1941). To what extent this revelation is a product of Clellan Ford's well-known anthropological interest in human sexual behavior is not known.

of her words, her accompanying gestures, her sometimes subtle, always gentle humor, which was often turned upon herself. Nani related her life history in English, interspersed with Haida words that I knew, and now and then she repeated an English sentence with its Haida equivalent.

Following my two trips in 1977, I returned twice to visit and work with Nani as the manuscript progressed through stages of completion. In August of 1978 I took with me the completed introductory chapters and rough version of her narrative. As I typed the narrative portions in July I was astounded at the growing list of questions I was amassing. The project had supposedly been completed the preceding summer, but I found I had neglected some basic life-cycle topics: how long mothers typically nursed their children, the significance of menopause for Haida women, the learning of sexual behavior, and others. In addition, I had enumerated questions dealing specifically with Nani's life history, such as whether the first children of Isabella and Charles Edenshaw had been born in a traditional house and where Isabella and Charles had lived after they were first married. Fortunately, I secured answers to most of my stock of questions during a week's return to Masset in August of 1978.

With the manuscript complete except for the Discussion and the Afterword, I returned in the summer of 1979 for another week. This time my main purposes were to check the large genealogy I had constructed and to read Nani's narrative to her. In addition, I sought her reflections on friendship, growing old, the changes she had witnessed, and the people she has admired. In July of 1980 I returned again, this time to work specifically with Nani on Haida kinship, but our tape recordings included some life-history data that have been incorporated into this narrative. My last visit with Nani before the book went to press, in July 1981, resulted in a few corrections and minor additions to the narrative.

ARCHIVAL RESEARCH

A considerable amount of ethnohistorical research both preceded and followed my fieldwork. In earlier trips to the Provincial Archives of British Columbia in Victoria I had surveyed most of the material relating to the nineteenth-century Haida, but had not explored extant twentieth-century materials. During July and August of 1977 and 1978 I researched these materials. Especially significant were two newspapers from the Queen Charlottes, the *Queen Charlotte Islander* and the *Masset Leader*, which were published during the second decade of the twentieth century. In addition to presenting local news, the *Islander* also ran a series of lengthy articles on the Haida during 1911, 1912, and 1913, written by Charles Harrison, a former missionary. Perusal of materials relating to Thomas Deasy, Indian agent at Masset from 1910 to 1924, revealed documents written by a Haida. Alfred Adams, Florence Davidson's uncle, carried on a regular correspondence with Deasy from 1924, when the latter left the Queen Charlottes, until the time of Deasy's death in 1936. Deasy's reports to the Minister of Indian Affairs, published in the annual reports from 1911 to 1920, present a detailed and generally sympathetic portrait of the Masset community.

From research conducted at the Church Missionary Society archives in 1972, I had compiled all the pertinent correspondence written by Masset missionaries from 1876 to 1913; some of this material has contributed to the present volume. The early marriage and baptismal records for St. John's Anglican Church at Masset, housed in the diocese headquarters in Prince Rupert, provided marriage dates for several of Florence Davidson's relatives and ancestors, documented Isabella Edenshaw's births prior to Florence, and pinpointed the baptismal dates for Florence and her sisters.

Ethnohistorical and ethnographic data have been drawn together to form the traditional and historic picture of Haida women in chapter 2. Additional data from more recent historical documents and from my own field journals are interspersed with Florence's narrative, both to lend a broader perspective to her account and to present a contemporary non-native view of the Haida.

CHAPTER 2

The Haida Woman

The women also to a great extent share the good qualities of the men. . . . They are exceedingly strong and can cut firewood, sail and paddle canoes, and work equally as hard as the men. They are all handsome and possess agreeable features when classed with the other coast Indians. [Harrison, April 29, 1912]

A Sketch of the Traditional People

They called themselves *Haada*, "people," and their world was divided into two islands, Haida Island (the Queen Charlottes) and the larger seaward country (the mainland). Both places were supported by a supernatural being, "Sacred One Standing and Moving," who in turn rested upon a copper box (Swanton 1909:12). The Haida population of some nine thousand was distributed among winter settlements located along the more protected shores and inlets of the Queen Charlotte Islands and, by the mid-eighteenth century, in southeastern Alaska. The large cedar-plank houses comprising these villages were built close together, nestled against the treeline and facing the beach in one or two long even rows. Above the storm-tide mark along the beachfront were erected the forest of totem poles so frequently remarked upon by nineteenth-century visitors to these remote shores. Advertising the greatness of their owners or owners' kin, some rested against the houses, some stood freely before the houses, and still others, shorter than the preceding types, contained the remains of the dead.

A maritime fishing, gathering, and hunting people, the Haida dispersed from March to November to resource areas where they fished, hunted sea and land mammals, gathered seaweed and other wild plants, and collected shellfish. The winter months, spent in the villages, were punctuated by the giving of potlatches and feasts, a prerogative of the wealthy.

Traditional Haida society was stratified into three categories: the *y'aʔ⹁Eyt* (nobles), the *ʔisʔaniya* (commoners), and the *həldənga* (slaves). This stratification was underpinned and reinforced by the ceremonial distribution of wealth and food in potlatching and feasting, respectively. The *y'aʔ⹁Eyt* were the "chiefs," the holders of high-ranking hereditary titles, the house owners, the wealthy, the ambitious, the clever, and the lucky. They were kind, generous, polite, and well-spoken; they fulfilled kinship obligations and had "respect for themselves." They gave potlatches and feasts to make good their names and to assure that their children would be y'aʔɕEyt, for the route to high status was through the potlatching efforts of one's parents. Ideally, this upper stratum of society exemplified all the desired and valued Haida qualities.

The ʔisʔaniya, on the other hand, were traditionally regarded as "kind of poor"; they did not show proper etiquette, did not exemplify "respect for self," talked "any old way," and were lazy. They were outnumbered by the y'aʔɕEyt. The həldənga were slaves or the descendants of slaves, captives taken in warfare or persons purchased as slaves from other tribes. They were without status, regarded as chattels, used as labor, and valued by their y'aʔɕEyt owners for the prestige their possession conveyed.

The Haida class division crosscut the descent organization of society. Descent was traced matrilineally, and named matrilineages, each headed by a chief, were the important resource-holding corporations. Lineages owned, among other properties, fishing streams, stretches of shoreline, stands of cedar trees, a corpus of hereditary names or titles, and "crests." The last, largely zoomorphic symbols, comprised the subject matter of most Haida art. Carved and painted on totem poles, feast dishes, chief's seats, frontlet headdresses, screens, housefronts, and canoe prows and paddles, among other items, crests symbolized the lineage affiliations of their owners.

The more than forty Haida lineages were grouped into two matrimoieties—Eagle and Raven—which, like the lineages, were exogamous, but unlike them, were not corporate. In addition to their marriage function, the moieties were ritually significant; one feasted and potlatched members of the opposite moiety and called upon them to perform mortuary functions. The larger significance of the Haida moiety division is exemplified in their classification of mythical beings and deities into this same dual schema.

Sources and Lacunae

There are several well-known ethnographic accounts of Haida culture, beginning with geologist George M. Dawson's 1878 study appended to the report of his geological survey of the Queen Charlotte Islands (Dawson 1880). Some thirty years later, John R. Swanton, a member of the Jesup Expedition of the American Museum of Natural History, conducted what still stands as the most

thorough investigation of traditional Haida culture. His extensive
Contributions to the Ethnology of the Haida (1909) was augmented a few
years later by the ethnography that Edward S. Curtis prepared in
1916 as part of his twenty-volume study of North American Indians.
Brief field research conducted in the summer of 1932 by G. P.
Murdock resulted in important additions to our understanding of
Haida social and ceremonial organization (Murdock 1934a, 1936).
Additionally, Murdock provided a summary of Haida culture
in *Our Primitive Contemporaries* (1934b). Ethnographic as well
as ethnohistorical data on Haida culture are also found in the
numerous accounts of eighteenth-century trading voyages to the
Queen Charlotte Islands (e.g., Bartlett 1925; Dixon 1789; Ingraham
1971; Marchand 1801), in the published and unpublished writings of
missionaries (e.g., Collison 1915; Harrison 1912–13; Harrison 1925),
government agents (e.g., Deasy 1911–20), and museum collectors
(e.g., Swan 1883).

Although the Haida have been well recorded in the ethnographic
literature, there are certain lacunae in this material. Perhaps most
importantly, ethnographic as well as historic sources on the Haida
chronicle a male world seen through the eyes of male writers, a bias
present in most earlier ethnographic literature from all areas of the
world. The lives of women are described primarily as they impinge
upon or complement the lives of men. Menstruation, pregnancy,
and childbirth, for example, had wide ramifying effects upon the
Haida community and consequently these aspects of the female
life cycle have been of sufficient interest to be reported in some
ethnographic detail. But what of girlhood, the learning of female
roles, the availability of power and authority to Haida women,
achievement in female terms; what of the experiences of aging,
menopause, and widowhood? We know little or nothing of these
cultural domains from the literature.

In short, the culture of Haida women has not been described. Yet,
in order for a life-history narrative to have meaning, one must
understand the traditions from which it derives. In this chapter I
draw together scattered data from ethnographic and historic sources
and from Florence Davidson's remarks upon Haida women in "the
olden days" to form a picture of the cultural position of traditional
Haida women. In particular I have dwelt upon the life cycle, the
division of labor, ceremonialism, and the value system. By the time
Florence Davidson was born, the Haida had been exposed to Euro-
American culture for over one hundred years and were considerably
acculturated in many respects. More changes followed during the
long years of Florence's marriage. These changes are also briefly

reviewed in this chapter, in terms of their effect upon the lives of Haida women.

THE LIFE CYCLE

Traditionally, the Haida preferred female to male children (Murdock 1934b: 248). Female children signified future expansion of the matrilineage, and their marriages brought males into the household to assist their fathers-in-law in "making canoes, fishing and hunting" (Harrison, November 25, 1912). On the other hand, it was important that a woman also have male children so that her brothers would have nephews to assist them and to succeed to their positions when they died.

Males and females were treated differently from the moment of birth. The umbilical cord of a baby girl was cut with a knife belonging to her mother; that of a boy was cut with the father's knife (Murdock 1934b: 248–49). Personal names (as opposed to honorific names) were bestowed in infancy and were sex linked. According to Murdock (1934: 249), the mother, after consultation with the child's father and grandparents, named a male infant after his real or classificatory paternal grandfather, while a female was named after one of her "grandmothers," a second-generation woman of the infant's own or the father's father's lineage. Harrison (November 25, 1912) notes that a shaman was often called in to determine which matrilineal ancestor had been reincarnated in the newborn and to name the infant accordingly.

While still infants, both males and females had their ears pierced, and, if of high rank, children of both sexes were tattooed on the arms, hands, and legs, and occasionally on the chest and back. It was customary, Harrison reports (December 16, 1912), for the parents to give small potlatches when their child was named, when its nose and ears were pierced, and again when it was tattooed.

The item of adornment that marked the Haida female, the labret or lip plug, was acquired during girlhood. An early maritime explorer (La Pérouse 1798: 165) remarks that all Haida women wore the labret, while most other ethnographers have claimed that the lip plug was a distinguishing mark of high-status women. Former missionary Charles Harrison described the procedure of insertion and the significance of the implement:

> . . . a hole is cut through the lower lip and an ivory or bone plug is inserted until the wound had healed. After healing the hole is stretched from time to time until it reached about half an inch in diameter and

about an inch in length. . . . These labrets are increased in size according to the rank of the person wearing them, and according to the number of children she had become the mother of. [Harrison, May 20, 1912]

A visible marker of both female status and high rank, the labret was evidently also symbolic of the emphasis the Haida placed upon female fecundity.

No formal restrictions seem to have been placed on the association of the sexes during childhood. Swanton (1909:60) mentions two games that were played together by boys and girls, but otherwise there are no ethnographic data on childhood play activities. Children's activities seemed to be generally sex segregated by Florence's time, as she noted that "boys played together and girls played together." Work activities during childhood were definitely sex differentiated and became more marked when a boy at age ten or eleven left his mother's household to reside with one of his mother's brothers. Under the tutelage of his mother's brother a boy received formal instruction in ceremonial roles and assisted his uncle in various economic activities. He was toughened by harsh discipline and rigorous physical activity.

Rigid and ritually maintained differences between the sexes began with a girl's puberty ceremony. The *tɔgwɔná*, or first menstruation seclusion, marked a very real change of life for a girl because, upon her emergence from this ritual seclusion, she was acknowledged to be a woman and was now marriageable. Charles Harrison described the ritual as follows:

> In the olden days when a girl reached maturity she had to pay strict attention to the order of the medicine man and pass through certain trying ordeals and ceremonies. A small tent was generally erected for her accommodation at the back of her father's house and in this tent she had to exist for fourteen days and sometimes longer.[1] Her face was generally painted and she had very little food given her. Should she during this period be compelled to go outside of her tent and accidentally meet a man, her face had to immediately be covered with her blanket. During this trying time she also wore a peculiar cloak made out of the inner bark of a cedar tree which covered her head and reached down to her knees, leaving only a small aperture for her eyes so that she could see where she was going. This cloak was only worn on this peculiar occasion so that when seen wearing this garb all the people looked upon her as about to pass from girlhood to womanhood.

1. Swanton (1909:48) and Curtis (1916:126) note that the period of seclusion was twenty days.

During the time she lived alone in the tent she was supposed to wear the robe both day and night. . . . When her time had expired and the doctor had given his consent the parents of the girl were accustomed to make a great feast and all the people in the village were invited to attend. When all were assembled the screen or the door of the tent was raised and the girl was seen sitting with her back to the guests dressed in the garb above referred to. This was removed by a woman authorized by the doctor to do this work and as soon as this sign of her degradation had disappeared the girl commenced to sing and dance before all the people present the songs and dances that she had been previously taught for this occasion. . . . After the feasting and congratulatory speeches were ended the rest of the night was spent in dancing. This custom has completely died away with the death of the last *Sa-ag-ga* [shaman].[2] [Charles Harrison, November 25, 1912]

During her seclusion a girl was visited exclusively by her female relatives—older sisters, mother, grandmother, and, perhaps most important, father's sisters (*sqaʔanlang*). From the latter she received formal instruction in womanly behavior: how to behave toward one's husband, how to rear children properly, standards of etiquette. Appropriate female behavior included submission, contentment, and industry (Dawson 1880:130B), endurance, modesty, a retiring disposition, and moderation in eating and drinking (Curtis 1916:126). Instruction and the various taboos enjoined upon the girl were designed to elicit these qualities.[3]

Childhood was both actually and symbolically terminated by the

2. Dawson (1880:131B) notes that the "coming out," described here by Harrison as involving a ceremony to which the entire village was invited, was a Tsimshian custom. He adds, "Similar customs probably exist among the Haidas, though I did not learn any details concerning them." Harrison, in his writings on the Haida, occasionally summarizes, or takes directly, passages from Dawson. I believe Dawson to be the source of Harrison's comment on the coming-out celebration, particularly as such a ceremony is not reported elsewhere in the Haida literature or mentioned by modern informants. I do not, however, believe that this ethnographic laxity on Harrison's part should be taken as a general indictment of Harrison's Haida material. Charles Harrison spent some twenty years among the Masset Haida, spoke the language fluently, and observed and recorded many aspects of traditional Haida culture.

3. Taboos and prescriptions included the following: no talking or laughing; no use of the regular house entrance; no looking at the house fire or the sea; no eating of fresh fish, seaweed, or shellfish; no contact with the hunting/fishing/gambling equipment of male household members; fasting and abstaining from drinking water (see Swanton 1909:49–50).

surrender of childhood toys and trinkets to the father's sisters during the period of seclusion (Murdock 1934b:250). At the end of her seclusion the girl's transition to womanhood was given public acknowledgment, as noted by Harrison above. Florence Davidson reported only that a small potlatch was given by the young woman's mother to women of the opposite moiety, particularly, and sometimes exclusively, to the young woman's father's sisters.

With menarche, the Haida female acquired a significant, if negative, power. Menstrual blood was considered extremely polluting. It could detrimentally affect shamanic powers, hunting and fishing equipment, the abundance of certain food resources, and a man's economic powers or his luck at gambling. Hunting, fishing, and gambling paraphernalia were kept outside a house in which a menstruating woman dwelled, and during her periods a woman was forbidden to walk in front of a man or step over salmon spawning creeks. Florence Davidson summed up Haida conceptions of this female power by remarking, "Once women change their life, they [men] are scared of them." She added, however, that a woman would not consider purposefully using this power against a man, though such uses of polluting power have been reported from a few other cultures (for example, see Strathern 1972: 255 for New Guinea).

Marriage usually followed shortly after the *təgwəná* seclusion. Murdock (1934a:359), Swanton (1909:50), and Harrison (November 25, 1912) credited a girl's mother with playing a decisive role in her marriage; according to Murdock, she arranged the marriage. Harrison contends that a young man took the initiative in selecting a prospective bride, but adds that the girl's mother had to approve. Though Murdock (1934b:251) notes that the wishes of the young couple received consideration in marriage arrangements, Florence Davidson's personal experience suggests that a young girl could not override the wishes of her elders. Also in Florence Davidson's case, somewhat contrary to the ethnographic accounts, marriage negotiations were between her husband-to-be (and his group) on the one hand, and her father and, ultimately, her maternal uncle, on the other.[4] According to Florence, traditionally as well as more recently, "the girl's uncle decided who she married. As long as your

4. In this case, Florence's maternal uncle was deferred to not only for traditional reasons but because, as an acculturated, enfranchised native knowledgeable in the ways of whites, it was hoped he could effect an accommodation of Haida tradition to white marriage practices.

uncle thinks it's all right, they all agree with him." The traditional marriage ritual that followed the negotiations is described in some detail by Swanton (1909:50–51).

Beyond the prescriptions of moiety and lineage exogamy, bilateral cross-cousin marriage was preferred: a girl would marry a real or classificatory father's sister's son or mother's brother's son.[5] Some pairs of Haida lineages reveal long histories of these preferred intermarriages. Several examples can be seen in Florence's genealogy. Residence after marriage was initially with the bride's parents because of the requirement of bride service; following that, residence was avunculocal, that is, with the husband's maternal uncle. In the event that the preferred pattern of cross-cousin marriage was followed, a girl would likely remain in her natal home for the duration of her marriage.

Polygyny was practiced but, according to all accounts, was not very common. Dawson, writing in 1878, noted that "[polygyny] was formerly more usual, but was always mainly or entirely confined to recognized chiefs. I could hear of but a single instance in which a man yet has two wives. . . . Three or four wives were not uncommon with a chief in former days . . ." (Dawson 1880:130B). There are no ethnographic data on the relationship between co-wives. Florence Davidson reports, however, that her "grandfather," Albert Edward Edenshaw, had two wives, the elder of whom was the mother's sister of the younger (see genealogy). His first wife encouraged him to take her sister's daughter as a second wife. The relationship between these two women was evidently quite harmonious.

According to Curtis (1916:121), most marriages were of relatively short duration. The separation of spouses (Curtis mentions only husband leaving wife) was common, and if a man simply left his wife, there was no redress. If a man mistreated his wife or abandoned her for another woman, however, he was held liable to her parents (in particular to her mother; see below). If a woman

---

5. Regular practice of bilateral cross-cousin marriage over the generations results in the genealogical merging of these two kin types; that is, father's sister's son is also mother's brother's son. In their description of Haida social structure, Rosman and Rubel distinguish between the marriages of chiefs and others, noting that the general preference was for marriage to father's sister's daughter and that the possibility of mother's brother's daughter marriage "appears to be restricted only to chiefs" (1971:39–40). My data do not suggest such strictly limited mother's brother's daughter marriage.

committed adultery, neither she nor her lover were accountable to her husband, though the latter might seek revenge. Rather, the lover was accountable to the woman's mother. Adultery was grounds for divorce among the Haida.

Large families were desired and it was expected that a woman would become pregnant within a few months following marriage. Florence Davidson noted that the inability to conceive was invariably blamed on the woman. When pregnant, a woman continued her routine daily activities, modified only by the observance of a number of taboos, almost all of which were designed to protect the developing fetus and assure an easy delivery. For the same reasons, the child's father and other household members were also subject to certain restrictions.[6] Parturition, according to Murdock (1934b:248), took place within the house, but according to Florence Davidson, women traditionally gave birth outside the house in a small hut specially constructed for the occasion. She noted, "They used to say they have the baby outside, not in the house because they have respect for their house keeping clean."[7] The afterbirth, soiled bedding, and clothing were later burned, and the mother remained in relative seclusion for ten days (Murdock 1934b:249).

Within the household, Murdock reports (1934b:252), a husband exerted but mild authority over his wife, which he was ashamed to show in the presence of others. Harrison, on the other hand, saw male authority as more decisive:

> The father was beyond any question master in his own house. To the mother belonged a peculiar domestic importance but both she and her children always obeyed the will of the actual lord of the household. The father was a master without being a tyrant; the mother was a subject without being a slave; and the children did not act in opposition to their parents' wishes. . . . [August 19, 1912]

6. Swanton gives examples of the "many things which a pregnant woman was not permitted to look at, and [the] many things which she must not eat" (1909:47). Taboos upon other household members included not playing with bows and arrows in the house (to avoid putting out the fetus' eyes). A pregnant woman's husband was enjoined from trifling talk with other women he was in love with, lest his wife should die. Florence Davidson adds that if the pregnant woman's husband slept with other women, the baby, out of jealousy, would refuse to be born.

7. That is, childbirth is polluting. The house is kept ritually clean by removing parturient women.

Harrison does not expound on a woman's "peculiar domestic importance," and the other ethnographic accounts offer no clues. Regarding the status of wives, Dawson, more in line with Murdock, notes that "the women appear to be well-treated on the whole, are by no means looked upon as mere servants, and have a voice in most matters in which the men engage" (1880:130B).

In her narrative, Florence Davidson remarks that a woman should have respect for her husband and look up to the men of the community as the leaders of the people. With age, however, appeared to come a measure of authority for a woman. A mother-in-law, for example, exerted some influence over her son-in-law who was expected not only to provide her and her husband with food but was required to pay her a considerable amount of property should he commit adultery. A woman could exact a similar property settlement from the suitor of her adulterous daughter (Swanton 1909:51). Following menopause, which apparently had none of the negative connotations it has in Euro-American society, a woman had access to cultural domains that were previously endangered by her menstrual periods (see sections, "Economics and the Division of Labor" and "Cultural Specialists," below). There was no Haida term specifically denoting the physiological experience of menopause; it was simply noted that when a woman reached a certain point in life, she ceased becoming pregnant. Florence observed that women who had had many children experienced no physical difficulties with menopause.

A married woman could hold property independently of her husband (Swanton 1909:54; Murdock 1934a:371) and a woman often received property from her parents as endowerment for her marriage. At her death her property was passed on to a daughter. Though a woman might continue to reside in her natal home following her marriage, the house itself and its name were considered male property; this had a critical effect upon the status of those widows who did not remarry.

Both the levirate (marriage to deceased husband's brother) and the sororate (marriage to deceased wife's sister) were traditionally practiced by the Haida. A man, however, had considerably more freedom in remarrying than a woman. A widower was required to give the mortuary potlatch for his deceased wife, and until he did so, he was beholden to his wife's family. It was preferred that a deceased woman's sister "take her chair" (the sororate) and her family would try to hold onto a man who had married into their lineage. Once a widower had given the mortuary potlatch, however, he was technically free to do as he pleased. A widow, on the other hand, was expected to marry a man of her husband's lineage, either a younger brother or a nephew. Late nineteenth-century church records and the recollections of Masset Haida indicate that the spouse was often quite junior to the widow. Florence's "grandmother," widow of Albert Edenshaw, is a case in point: two years following Edenshaw's death in 1894, she was married to one of her husband's nephews (Phillip White), who at age twenty-four was some twenty years younger than she. Although an older widow exerted considerable influence over her young husband, who "was just like a slave to his uncle's wife," she had little or no voice in the selection of her new husband. Florence Davidson recounted one such levirate marriage which dates from the mid-nineteenth century:

> Taɫanat married an old, old lady, his uncle's wife. He was about ten or eleven and was out playing while they prepared for the wedding. His mother called him home, washed the mud off his feet, and put a shirt on him. "You're going to stay with that old lady, your uncle's wife." But he didn't understand. His mother took him inside to the top step [of the housepit] and sat him beside the old woman on a pillow. All the food—smoked dog salmon soaked in salt water—was served. "Eat, dear, eat," the old lady said to him, but he didn't want to eat. "I wonder why that old thing said that to me," he asked. "Look at all my granddaughters, those pretty girls. I'll die quick and you'll marry one of them." He looked at the girls and he hated them. The old lady was supposed to let her new husband sleep by her, but he didn't want it. Maybe when it started to get cold out he started sleeping by the old woman.

The levirate was really the only security a widowed woman had, for a widow who did not remarry was often left destitute. She was not allowed to stay in her former husband's home, and, if lucky, she escaped with a few personal belongings when her husband's heir took over the house and its property. Masset people cited several instances when widows hurriedly left their former husbands' houses and, with their children, sought sanctuary in the homes of matrilineal relatives. These women were pitied and high-ranking people were instructed to be kind to them and offer them food. Widowers, as noted above, did not suffer a symmetrical fate.

Mourning rituals were identical for widow or widower (Murdock 1934a:373). The grieving spouse remained isolated for a period of time and ate very little because, in Florence Davidson's words, "if they think nothing of it [death], there's no luck. You have to deny yourself." Mortuary potlatches were given for both men and women of high rank.

Economics and the Division of Labor

Although some economic activities, such as collecting shellfish and cooking, were performed by both males and females, in general the Haida division of labor was marked. Men might beachcomb during the winter following onshore storms to collect clams and cockles that had washed ashore, but clam digging and the implement of procurement, the *gǐigú* (digging stick), were considered part of a woman's domain. The sexual division of labor was summed up for me by one elderly Masset man who offered the following comment on the essential property of a newly married couple: "Every man's got to have his fishing line and devilfish stick and every woman her digging stick."

The gathering of plant resources was women's and girls' work; young boys did not normally accompany their mothers on such expeditions. What little gathering men did complemented that of the women. Both sexes, for example, collected spruce roots, but women dug the small delicate roots for hat and basket weaving, and men the large roots from which they made fish traps and snares. Similiarly, both men and women collected cedar bark, but women sought the inner bark for weaving mats, and men the large sheets of outer bark for roofing.

Women's abstention from certain economic activities seems to have been rationalized and prohibited on the basis of pollution taboos associated with menstruation and reproduction (see, for example, Swanton 1909:219). Fishing lines and hooks, sea mammal clubs, bows, arrows, and any other items of subsistence technology used by males were kept outside the house, concealed from the view of female household members. Menstruating women were believed to have supernatural visual powers capable of causing considerable damage. Were a menstruating woman to see a man's fishing or hunting equipment, all of his economic endeavors would be doomed. If a woman were to attempt to hunt or fish herself, her efforts would go similarly unrewarded. For this reason, the Haida say, women never fished or hunted. Nor did women collect octopuses, comestible shellfish but more commonly used as halibut bait. Were a woman to catch an octopus near its rocky den, all octopuses would permanently abandon the site.

Male economic activities could be further influenced by domestic activities. Baby tending, for example, was fraught with potential ruination of male economic prowess. A man might play with his small children, but his handling of a soiled or wet baby would diminish his luck at hunting or fishing, perhaps spelling economic disaster for the entire household. To assure the ritual purity of male members of the household, men's clothing was washed separately from that of women and children. Ritual cleanliness brought economic rewards, for "those who were 'clean' were blessed with food and riches," according to Florence Davidson. Men could negatively affect their own economic endeavors by having extramarital affairs or by leaving their wives. A man who did so would lose his luck at hunting or fishing. Ritual purity and consequent economic "luck" were also acquired or enhanced by drinking medicine,[8] a male prerogative. Women, too, drank medicine, but only to cure sickness, not for "luck."

The sexual division of labor in trading is not clear. Swanton (1909) and Curtis (1916) make no mention of women in trading; Murdock (1934b:377), in his brief discussion of trading partnerships, implies that the parties are male but does not discuss trade more generally. Early maritime traders' accounts from the late eighteenth century, however, suggest that Haida women played a significant and authoritative role in trading activities at the time of first contact. In his journals of 1790–92, Joseph Ingraham, for example, offers the following comment:

> Here in direct opposition to most other parts of the world, the women maintain a precedency to the men in every point insomuch as a man dares not trade without the concurrence of his wife. Nay, I have often been witness to men being abused by their wives for parting with skins before their approbation was obtained. [Ingraham 1971:132]

The men of the ship *Columbia Rediviva* similarly remarked on the ascendant role of Haida women in trade:

> The women in trade, as well as in everything else which came within our knowledge, appeared to govern the men; as no one dared to conclude a bargain without first asking his wife's consent; if he did, the moment he went into his canoe he was sure to get a beating . . . and there is no mercy to be expected without the intercession of some kind female. [Howay 1941:208]

Howay adds in a footnote that "all witnesses agree on this" (1941:208). On the basis of the above and similar evidence from the late eighteenth century, it seems quite possible that women played a significant role in trading, particularly as they could hold property independently of their husbands. Given the acknowledged role of

8. Florence could not specify the type of "medicine" drunk.

men as traders, however, it may be that they represented their wives in exchange and that the dominant role of women reflects the latter's interest in their own property.

Dawson downplayed the general economic contribution of Haida women, noting that ". . . the women do not contribute materially to the support of the family, attending only to the accessory duties of curing and preserving the fish . . ." (1880:130B). Swanton suggests the symbolic importance of woman's freedom from economic activities in the following remark: "A young, unmarried woman was not allowed to do much work, and lay in bed a great deal of the time. This was so that she might marry a chief, and always have little work to do" (1909:50). From Florence Davidson's comments it seems unlikely that even a high-ranking woman would actually have little work to do. Though she might have slaves to gather firewood and assist in the processing of fish and other foods, the desire for prestige and the ambition characteristic of the Haida spurred all toward the accumulation of wealth and surplus resources. Florence's remark that "we try all our best for our children" applies equally to the aboriginal Haida whose paramount concern was securing a place for their children in the social order. Neither is Dawson's comment that women do not contribute materially to the support of the family an accurate assessment of the economic position of Haida women. The ability of a woman to process foods, particularly fish, was of considerable concern to all. A woman adept at slicing and drying fish was greatly admired for her skills. Furthermore, the limitations on the quantity of salmon a household could garner for winter stores was dependent not upon the number of fish that men could catch but on the number that women could practicably clean, slice, and dry. Thus female skills were critical to the ability of a household to provision itself and to lay aside a surplus for feasting and potlatching.

Ceremonial Division of Labor

Men and women also filled complementary roles in ceremonialism. Both sexes hosted potlatches, though the house-building (*waɫəɫ*) and mortuary (*sik'*) potlatches were normally sponsored by males,[9] and the *təgwəná* (female puberty potlatch) was an exclusively female

9. Murdock (1936:12) argues that a woman (the wife of the new house owner) was the actual host of the *waɫəɫ* potlatch. Rosman and Rubel (1971:57–64), following Swanton (1909), present a convincing argument that the man was the potlatch host. I have suggested elsewhere that while

event. Either a man or a woman might give a vengeance (*gədáng*) or face-saving (*ˤansəngáda*) potlatch, as these were precipitated by some impertinence shown the individual or some embarrassment suffered, regardless of sex.

Both men and women were recipients of potlatch wealth and, as children at their father's potlatches, received equal attention in the form of tattoos and honorific names. A woman might be selected to perform ceremonial labor at a potlatch, such as the preparation of new house timbers. Though her husband actually performed the work in her stead, she would receive the payment for the service (Murdock 1936:5).

Potlatches were the only occasions when high-ranking individuals were initiated into the dancing societies, which were attenuated versions of Northern Kwakiutl dances acquired from the Tsimshian in the eighteenth century (see Swanton 1909:156–76). Depending on the source consulted, the Haida had between six and eleven such dances. Curtis (1916:142) noted that "women were barred from the more important dances," and Swanton's catalogue of dances by the sex of the performers (1909:161) concurs with Curtis' generalization.

Murdock describes several other dances that punctuated potlatch celebrations but in these the sexual division was not so marked, though in one dance (*sɑ'adal*) only the men carried rattles (1936:4). Dawson adds, however, that "the women occupy a prominent place in this dance, being carefully dressed with the little marks [?] and *nax-in* [Chilkat blankets] . . . previously described" (1880:128B). Women could wear the chief's headdress, or *amalahait*, a frontlet bearing a carved crest figure, encircled with sea lion whiskers (containing eagle down), and trailing numerous ermine pelts. The *amalahait* and Chilkat blanket were worn in the dance performed by high-ranking men and women as a welcome to visitors. This dance was still being performed when Florence Davidson was a child.

Women's traditional roles in feasting are not clear. Murdock (1934a:364–65) cites evidence indicating that women not only attended but hosted feasts at which males were present. Swanton's description of the *sik'* potlatch implies that both males and females were guests at Haida feasts (1909:176–80), and Charles Harrison's accounts from 1911 to 1913 indicate the same. Florence Davidson, on

---

the male role may receive the most emphasis, the *waɬɬ* may be interpreted as hosted by a man and his wife (Blackman 1977:45). It is worth mentioning, however, that even Murdock (1936:19) notes that a woman could not hold a *waɬɬ* for her children by herself.

the other hand, stated that, prior to her time, only the men used to attend and host feasts and that attendance at feasts by couples is a relatively recent practice inaugurated during her early childhood. The attendance of feasts by couples also points to the breakdown of moiety organization, for traditionally one only feasted members of the opposite moiety. Regardless of the discrepancy in these accounts, it is clear that the participation of women in feasting increased dramatically in the twentieth century.[10]

The most important ceremonial role a woman played was as a *sqaʔan*, a father's sister (or, more generally, a female of father's lineage). This role was not matched by any comparable male ritual role. The *sqaʔan* was a focal person in the lives of her brother's children from the moment of their birth to their placement in the grave. She cut the umbilical cord, was the ritual if not actual tattooer of the children, tended to her brother's daughters during their puberty seclusion and witnessed their emergence into womanhood. Regardless of whether her brother's son married her own daughter, she was present at the marriage to usher the bride to her nephew's side, and, according to Murdock (1934b:364), she gave the wedding feast. Her own name might eventually be passed on to her brother's son's daughter. A *sqaʔan* tended her brother's children when they were ill and fulfilled her final ritual duty in the life cycle of a brother's child by preparing the body at death and keeping a mourning vigil for four days. Today the modern legacy of this final ritual act is realized when the deceased's *sqaʔan* washes off the headstone before it is placed on the grave.

Cultural Specialists

Positions of household and external authority—house, lineage, and town chieftainships—were regarded as male positions, though aboriginal examples of women chiefs are not unknown. Curtis, for example, recounting a legendary war between the west coast and southernmost Haida, notes that the chief of the Do-hade, or West Coast, people was a "great fat woman" (1916:172). The assumption of chieftainships by women became more common in late post-contact times. Dawson, in this regard, notes that "only recently and because of the depletion of the population have women succeeded to the seats of nobility" (1880:118B). Florence Davidson concurred, noting that women assumed chieftainships only when there were no

---

10. Susan Kenyon notes that the same has happened in the Westcoast (Nootka) community of Kyuquot (personal communication).

male heirs. Masset people recalled one instance from the late nineteenth century when a woman assumed a lineage chieftainship only because there was no male to take the position; when her own son became an adult, the position was passed on to him. Harrison reports a potlatch given at the raising of the last totem pole in Masset, which stood before the house of a woman chief named Kitkune (see genealogy): "Thousands of dollars worth of blankets, crockery, guns, bracelets, coins and goods of all descriptions were given to testify to the fact that this woman was indeed a great, wealthy, and important chieftess" (September 9, 1912). Traditionally, not only would the position have been occupied by a man, but the potlatch would have been hosted by a male. Women did, however, regularly participate in lineage councils in aboriginal times (Murdock 1936:17), and accordingly had a voice in the selection of successors to lineage and town chieftainships. Unfortunately, these powers are not detailed in the ethnographic literature.

Harrison notes a special role filled only by old women who were paid mourners at funerals.

> These were generally the witches of the tribe that did this work and also assisted the devil doctor at births in his search to locate definitely what ancestor's soul had taken possession of the newly born child's body. These old women acted the part of *accouchers* [sic] at births and washed and dressed the corpses for burial and consequently were looked upon with great respect. [December 2, 1912]

Though Harrison mentions only old women as shamanic assistants in the above account, shamanism was a specialty open to both Haida males and females. Most ethnographic accounts, however, imply that practitioners were, as a rule, males, and one might suspect that unless past menopause a female shaman would be at a certain disadvantage. As Curtis remarks: "Females except old women and girls under the age of puberty were barred from the house in which a shaman was at work lest someone in her periods blight his power" (1916:137). The literature, however, does not indicate that female shamans must be past the climacteric, nor is there any reason to believe that female shamanic powers were in any way diminished from those of males. Florence Davidson, in fact, recalled a woman shaman from her childhood who commanded the respect of the village because she had predicted World War I long before its occurrence.

In aesthetic specialties there were marked male/female differences. What is normally regarded as Haida "art" was traditionally a masculine art. The painting or carving of mythological or crest figures were male prerogatives. This division of aesthetic labor serves to explain why women assigned the ritual task of tattooing a brother's child delegated the task to a male (see Murdock 1936:8; Curtis 1916:125): tattoos were crest art.

Women's art, by contrast, was geometric, confined to the decorative weaving of spruce roots and cedar bark. It derived from natural forms (the "snail's track," for example, was a common hat brim pattern), not from mythological or sociological sources. Zoomorphic and anthropomorphic crest designs were not a woman's domain, and this division of aesthetic labor has persisted well into the twentieth century. Button blankets, for instance, were and are designed by men, though cut and appliquéd by women. Under unusual circumstances a woman might paint crest and other male designs. Florence's mother, Isabella, for example, painted designs on the spruce root hats she wove after her artist husband's death, and Florence herself designed and painted the prow of a canoe built by her husband and his brother in the 1930s. As noted in her narrative (chap. 9), however, she felt uncomfortable in the role of artist: "I just painted once, on that big canoe. I never tried to carve; I thought it was meant to be for men. No women carved or painted during my time; they were all weaving."

Cultural Values

Haida women were valued as perpetuators of the lineage and it was anticipated that a woman would bear many children (ten, a ritually significant number, was mentioned as an ideal by Florence Davidson). The reproductive power a woman possessed was natural, not cultural (Rosaldo 1974:30). Women had life-giving (bearing children) or death-bringing (causing the death of a husband in warfare) powers because of their physiological functions; these powers developed as they matured but could not be actively sought. Men, on the other hand, had culturally bestowed powers, acquired through observing prescriptions (drinking medicine, following certain hunting rules) and proscriptions (avoiding female powers). Female power was serendipitous in effect, controlled and confined by observance of taboos, but not manipulated to effect results.

The marked pollution taboos that colored relationships between males and females may have been in part rationalized on the grounds that Haida women were believed to be the sexual aggressors. In this regard, James Deans emphatically states that "their women considered it their duty to encourage at all times sexual intercourse" (1891:23). Unfortunately, other early Haida ethnographers are silent on the details of sexual behavior.[11] Florence Davidson's account suggests only that young women may have been relatively ignorant of sex; if sexual aggressiveness was characteristic of traditional Haida women, it must have developed after some years of postmarital sexual experience. Assuming Deans is correct in his statement, the taboos enjoined upon women could have served to contain and confine potentially disruptive female sexual aggressiveness.[12]

In other respects, however, women were regarded as far from aggressive. As previously noted, among the desirable qualities inculcated in young females were modesty and a retiring disposition. Harrison's admiration for the physical strength of Haida women notwithstanding (see epigraph to chap. 2), women were regarded as the weaker sex both mentally and physically. "If women want to do anything, they [men] thought they can't do it," Florence Davidson explained in regard to the competence of women.

But there was room for individual variation from this norm. Coming from a family with a dearth of males, Florence was instructed by her father and her mother's brother: "Don't be hopeless, like a girl." Perhaps because she heeded their advice, Florence Davidson became the very strong and respected woman that she is today.

CULTURE CONTACT AND SEX ROLES

Contact with Euro-Canadian and American culture wrought both subtle and profound changes in traditional Haida sex roles. These changes were not necessarily uniform; the status of women was differentially affected by the various agents, events, and processes of culture change. The early maritime trade of the late eighteenth century and the subsequent Hudson's Bay Company-dominated trade, the contact culture experienced in Victoria, wage labor, the dramatic population decline of the 1860s and 1870s, missionization, and the Indian Act, all contributed in varying ways to reshaping the role of Haida women.

11. Murdock does discuss "semi-sanctioned" extra-marital sexual relationships and sanctioned premarital relationships (1934a:364, 375–76). The latter contrasts with Florence Davidson's discussion of the protection of adolescent females.

12. Wanton female sexuality is a rationalization in a number of cultures for the avoidance and control of females by males.

Maritime Trade, 1785–1825

Maritime trader accounts cited earlier stressed the preeminent role of Haida women in trading. Other features of this early trade with Euro-Americans, however, point to the clearcut dominance of native males in the trading economy of the late eighteenth and early nineteenth centuries. First, the trade was based on the exchange of sea otter furs. While the processing of these furs was a female task, the hunting of sea otter was a prestigious and ritually imbued activity of high-ranking males. So also were the formalities of trading. One has only to consider the intensity and magnitude of the trade to see how significantly it loomed in the lives of the Haida, particularly Haida males. Wike (1951:10) estimates that during about a twenty-five-year period, American traders (the most active in the trade) acquired 350,000 otter pelts from the natives along the coast, the bulk of which came from Haida and Westcoast (Nootka) territories. In return the natives received some seven million dollars worth of goods. As the foreign demand for otter pelts grew, the Haida diverted increasing amounts of energy from other activities into hunting, processing, and trading sea otter furs. This demand probably affected males more than females as the former were both the hunters and the primary traders.

The variety of goods introduced to the natives likewise suggests a male emphasis in the trading economy. Though flour, cloth, kettles and other utensils, and decorative items, such as Chinese coins, mirrors, and thimbles, could be counted as women's goods, the staple items of the trade—iron tools and guns—were male goods. In sum, the maritime trade might be viewed from an economic perspective as having stimulated male domains of Haida culture, though not necessarily at the expense of female domains.

In another respect, however, the maritime trade may have contributed to the degradation of Haida and other Northwest Coast women. Women were offered to white traders, perhaps as part of the ritual exchange between the trading parties. Spanish explorer Jacinto Caamaño, for example, noted in 1792 that "the natives were greatly surprised at our abstaining from any commerce with their women, whom they brought with them, so we understood, for that purpose, since they are accustomed to the English and others who trade in these parts, not only accepting, but also demanding, and choosing them" (Wagner and Newcombe 1938:207).

Caamaño's remark is verified by another account, from the ship *Eliza*. Describing events at the village of Kiusta in the northwest corner of the Queen Charlotte Islands, the log keeper relates: "The old woman proceeded to the last offer of friendship, which was a lady for the night, out of her numerous seraglio, with which she accommodates all vessells (sic) that stop here" (cited in Duff n.d.). Caamaño's account suggests that women offered by trading chiefs were not of high rank but were perhaps slaves. Anchored at the village of Dadens on North Island in 1792, he reports that he was offered the chief's daughter "so that I might enjoy her." It seems doubtful that the girl in question was the chief's daughter as Caamaño adds, "She had no tablet [labret] in in her lower lip and was quite pleasing in appearance" (Wagner and Newcombe 1938:207). The social status of women mentioned in other accounts is not clear.

The negative effects of late eighteenth- and early nineteenth-century prostitution are pointedly noted by Jonathan Green, a Methodist missionary who visited the Queen Charlottes and southeastern Alaska in 1829, just after the decline of the sea otter trade. Green remarks that he learned from a Kaigani (Alaskan) Haida chief "that all the young women of the [Kaigani] tribe visit ships for the purpose of gain by prostitution, and in most cases destroy their children, the fruit of this infamous intercourse" (1915:68).

After the turn of the nineteenth century the economic position of Haida women was likely affected by the addition of the potato to the native economy. Introduced by traders in the late eighteenth century, the potato was intensively cultivated by Queen Charlotte Haida women, and by the 1840s several hundred bushels were being traded annually to the Tsimshian and the Hudson's Bay Company at Fort Simpson (Dunn 1846:41). The potato trade for the Haida was relatively short-lived, however, when after 1850 potato cultivation was undertaken by Hudson's Bay Company employees at Fort Simpson.

The Contact Culture in Mid-century Victoria

By the late 1850s the Haida were increasingly frequenting Victoria where they traded at the Hudson's Bay Company post, availed themselves of a supply of illegal liquor from "whiskey traders," traded and feuded with local as well as other northern native groups, and found themselves entangled in scuffles with the law. Along with groups of Tlingit and Tsimshian, as many as several hundred Haida wintered over in Victoria encamped in the vicinity of the Hudson's Bay Company post. These migrations must have disrupted winter village life as large numbers of natives, normally resident in winter settlements on the Queen Charlottes, now opted for a winter of urban squatting. Though ceremonial patterns that were part of village life may have carried over to the urban camps, there is no reporting of Haida ceremonial activities in the local Victoria newspaper, the *British Colonist*.

The white populace of Victoria became increasingly concerned with the large encampments of natives on the edge of town and various attempts were made to confine and curtail native activities. Many northern native women, however, spent much of their time within the town limits where they staffed the "dance halls," or houses of prostitution. Unfortunately, little mention is made of prostitution in the newspapers, save the occasional arrest of a streetwalker. Francis Poole, a civil and mining engineer who explored the Queen Charlotte Islands during 1862–63, suggests that prostitution offered certain advantages to Haida women:

> Not only does no dishonour attach to that degrading practice, but if successful in making money, it is highly honoured. I remember one singular case of this. Some Queen Charlotte women went to spend the Winter at Victoria, hoping to "earn blankets." They came back loaded with blankets, trinkets, tobacco, whiskey, and other presents, which they proceeded to distribute among their people. . . . [Poole 1872:312–13]

Though evidently in some instances new economic wealth from prostitution allowed women to participate independently in potlatching, other writers of the time, such as Krause (1885:207) and Jackson (1880:118), paint a much grimmer picture, which emphasizes the exploitation of native women by both native and white men. Jackson, for example, describes the fate of Kaigani Haida and Tlingit women: "They are sometimes . . . sent to the mines, while the husband lives in idleness at home on the wages of their immorality." In the long run, the effects of prostitution were disastrous, for the tolls exacted in population costs far offset any immediate economic gains. Wilson Duff describes the general trend: "Venereal disease, a result of prevalent prostitution, killed many and rendered infertile many more" (1964:43).

Life in Victoria and large-scale prostitution came to an end in the years following the smallpox epidemic of 1862. Introduced by a miner from San Francisco, the disease had a devastating effect upon the vulnerable, unvaccinated natives but left the white population of the area virtually untouched. Florence Davidson's narrative touches on the personal tragedy of the smallpox epidemic.

The Population Decline and After

The population decline resulting from the smallpox epidemic was swift and dramatic in its proportions. By 1885 the Haida population was down to 13 percent of its former numbers (Duff 1964:39). This reduction had a significant effect upon the status of women, who, on the one hand, found their traditional roles of childbearing and rearing ever more critical as numerous lineages were threatened with extinction, while on the other hand, they began assuming positions of authority outside the domestic realm, taking up chieftainships when there were no male heirs to fill the positions. The ascendancy they may have enjoyed as chiefs, however, was short-lived. The combined effects of the Indian Act,[13] which allowed for a system of elected band councilors, the Indian Reserve Commission, which divided up lineage land holdings, and the missionaries, who persuaded several leading chiefs to forego potlatching, conspired to reduce the power and authority of the hereditary chiefs (see Blackman 1977 for discussion of these factors). Furthermore, as previously noted, a woman chief was regarded as an anomaly and every effort was made to transfer the position to a male.

The missionaries who arrived among the Haida in 1876 brought to the native culture a domestic structure which more accurately reflected that of the acculturating society. Heretofore, white women had not really been part of the contact culture, except perhaps peripherally in Victoria. But missionaries came to the native communities with wives and families. Though the culture and religion they brought were patriarchal, several of the changes they wrought among the Haida affected the status of native women positively. The missionary wife, for example, created a special interest group of Haida women. An auxiliary to the newly founded mission church, the "White Cross *jade* [women]" regularly met for Bible readings, hymn singing, sewing, and handiwork, put on basket socials to raise money for the church, tended to the dead, and assisted bereaved families. The group later evolved into the Women's Auxiliary of the Anglican Church (today the Anglican Church Women). The founding of this social group set up a communication network among community women which had not existed previously.

13. The Indian Act, originally enacted in 1876 and revised several times (most recently in 1951), is a sweeping piece of legislation outlining the

Masset in 1879 (photograph by O. C. Hastings, courtesy, Glenbow-Alberta Institute)

Ceremonial patterns were also greatly altered by the missionaries (see Blackman 1973, 1977). For example, the Anglican missionaries undercut the male emphasis present in feasting. They stressed commensality among men and women and set an example by inviting couples to the mission house to dine. Now in the 1980s, feasts are typically hosted by married couples. One missionary, J. H. Keen, attempted in the 1890s to break the pattern of feasting large numbers of guests by encouraging only small dinner parties. The feasting complex held sway, however, though superficially it came to resemble the Sunday mission-house dinners. By the end of the nineteenth century, feasts were given not only for traditional reasons (taking and keeping the chief's place, marriage, death), but also in celebration of Christian holidays. A significant material cultural change was a factor in the acculturation of feasting and in the increasingly important role women came to play in it. Traditional feasting utensils—carved spoons, grease bowls, and the larger carved feast bowls—were men's property, created by male artists and carvers for male patrons. These items were replaced in the latter part of the nineteenth century by bone china, silverware, and tablecloths, all women's property.

Cultural changes of the late nineteenth century also included the

Canadian government's responsibilities to and control over Canadian Indian bands.

expanded participation of women in the potlatching complex. This can be seen as the result of two seemingly opposing phenomena. On the one hand, the hosting of the potlatches by women is a logical consequence of their assumption of chieftainships, and is, therefore, traditional. On the other hand, women's more active roles in potlatching were a product of acculturation, possibly related to Anglican influences on the traditional mortuary potlatch and very definitely linked to changes in marriage patterns. I suspect that the active role women played in the church as fundraisers and sponsors of social events carried over to their assumption of more active roles in Anglicized mortuary potlatches as organizers, as speechmakers, and, eventually, as hosts. This was facilitated by the abolishment of the levirate and changes in inheritance patterns promoted by Reverend Charles Harrison, missionary at Masset in the early 1880s. Harrison recognized that traditional marriage practices discriminated against widows. As noted earlier, an unremarried widow was customarily forced to vacate her deceased husband's home and seek refuge in a house owned by her own lineage. Many of these widows were not only dependent but destitute. As a result of missionary efforts and, later, the application of the Indian Act, women were allowed a share of their husbands' estates. This, in turn, has provided the means for the participation of elderly women, such as Florence Davidson, in the ceremonial complex.

By no means did all missionary endeavors or all government decisions pertaining to the Haida improve the status of women. After all, agents of both the church and the government were male members of a male-dominant society. The Indian Act, as a product of that society, is a classic case in point. Several writers, most recently Kathleen Jamieson (1978), have pointed out that the Indian Act, particularly in its definition of band membership, is flagrantly biased against native women. It revokes band membership from native women marrying whites or non-status natives and denies band membership to the subsequently born offspring of these women. Simultaneously the Act confers band membership on white wives of male band members and on the offspring born of such marriages. The noticeable rise in premarital births among the Haida during the twentieth century (Stearns 1981) may be in part attributable to this sex discriminatory feature of the Indian Act. Having children out of wedlock has been an intentional strategy on the part of some Haida women whose mates are not band members.[14]

14. Mitchell (1976:383) suggests that the same strategy has been employed by Coast Salish women.

By not marrying, a woman can keep her band membership and enroll her children on the band list.

The changes that occurred in the female puberty potlatch (təgwəná) are illustrative of further negative effects of the infliction of Victorian values upon a native society. By the 1920s the puberty potlatch and its attendant seclusion had ceased. The former significance of this potlatch for Haida women is exemplified in the last large təgwəná given—for a girl who at age seventeen had not yet begun to menstruate. The girl's mother believed the rite of passage so important that she gave the potlatch anyway and, as if to compensate for what everyone knew had not occurred, invited men as well as women and distributed large quantities of property. When I asked her why the Haida discontinued the təgwəná, Florence Davidson replied, "They became ashamed of it." As in many other traditional cultures, menstruation, while dangerous and powerful, was not regarded as shameful by the Haida. In traditional Haida society, the monthly seclusions, the concealment of the hunting and fishing gear, the active avoidance of male possessions by menstruating women, and the təgwəná celebration were all public advertisements of femaleness. Menstruation was not cloaked in secrecy; rather, public knowledge of it was to everyone's advantage. The repression of these pollution taboos and the consequent repression of natural female power are reflective of the Haida adoption of Euro-Canadian values, the values of a Victorian and patriarchal society.

Missionary emphasis upon nuclear family units and the government's Indian Act affected the status of women by gradually eroding matrilineal descent. Although today matrilineal descent is still acknowledged to exist by the older generation and is traced for certain purposes, bilateral English kin terms prevail, lineage exogamy is no longer practiced, and most younger people do not know their lineage membership. Moiety affiliation is generally known and functions on ceremonial occasions, though moiety exogamy has also broken down. Application of the Indian Act early in the twentieth century furthered this trend by altering traditional patterns of matrilineal inheritance and wresting traditional authority from the lineage and placing it in the hands of an elected group of band councilors. With the undercutting of lineage authority, women lost the formal input they once had into the political realm of lineage councils. Elected band councilors have almost invariably been male, resulting, I suspect, in a considerable decline of female input into community and band politics. In the ceremonial realm, however, the input of older women is still considerable, as they play an active role in the planning and execution of feasts and potlatches. Florence Davidson's role in the pre-potlatch meetings for Oliver Adams' installation as town chief is exemplary of this function of older women (see chap. 9).

Florence Davidson's narrative suggests that during the twentieth century women have become more domestically isolated than traditionally. Though the Haida population was still quite mobile in the early years of Florence's marriage as evidenced in the fact that people left the village to work in mainland canneries, camped with families at North Island, or traveled upriver for salmon, Florence lamented that having a large family often kept her tied to the house. She had no time for clam digging, for example, and viewed as a holiday the opportunity to leave the house for a few hours to help with the hard work of preparing a feast. With decreasing reliance on native foods, women became more homebound, and expeditions to collect seaweed, chitons, wild rhubarb, and other foods became luxuries, not necessities.

Traditional ideas about the domestic division of labor were not all that incongruous with the division of labor in white society. Nonetheless, Indian agent and missionary families provided new role models for male/female relationships. That white ideals were absorbed, at least by some Haida, fairly early in the twentieth century is indicated in the following speech Florence's uncle, Henry Edenshaw, gave at the wedding of his eldest daughter in 1913:

> . . . I have done my utmost to act in my family as a White man, and my children, when of a suitable age, have been sent to the White children's school to finish their education. . . . The ideals concerning excellence in men and women's character have always risen or fallen together. . . . it has often been assumed that next to the Christian religion, humanity has no other so precious inheritance as Shakespeare's divine gallery of womanhood which I hope my daughter, now Mrs. Nash, will inspire and follow. The books that I have read teach me that during the past fifty years the ideals of womanly excellence and of marriage have risen, and that the practical observance of those ideals by men has risen and is likely to rise.

Perhaps more a reflection of the changing status of Haida art than of the changing status of Haida women are the inroads females have made into the once exclusively male visual arts. Paralleling, but not necessarily caused by, the evolution of Haida art from ceremonial to commercial, has been the emergence of women argillite, wood, and silver carvers and graphics artists. In 1977, following a meeting of Haida artists at Florence Davidson's home, I wondered though just how much women's roles had changed when I found myself

together with a woman artist in the kitchen doing the dishes and
discussing the maternal themes prevalent in her art.

THE STATUS OF HAIDA WOMEN: A SUMMARY

A common theme running through the analysis of matrilineal
societies is that women enjoy, if not external authority, culturally
favorable status simply by virtue of the fact that descent is traced
through females who are seen as the focus of the entire social
structure (Martin and Voorhies 1975:224–25). Quinn's review of the
data (1977:211–14), on the contrary, brings together evidence that
the status of women in matrilineal societies is a function of several
variables, among them residence patterns, the organization of the
domestic group, and the division of domestic authority. In the case
of the Haida, the decision-making powers women had in lineage
councils, their property-holding rights, and the potential for female
succession to chieftainships can all be related to an ideology of
matrilineal descent. Other variables which suggest a lowering
of female status (personality attributes, physical and mental
inferiority to men, pollution taboos) can perhaps be seen as indirect
consequences of the status benefits of matrilineal descent. In this
respect, Quinn remarks that "male dominance myths, far from
reflecting women's overall low status, arise precisely because women
have considerable economic importance, personal autonomy, and
domestic influence" (1977:219).

In her review of the anthropological literature dealing with
women's status, Quinn has pointed out, furthermore, that the status
of women may vary within a culture, being relatively high in some
cultural domains and low in others. It may also fluctuate throughout
the life cycle. For the Haida female, status was perhaps lowest at the
time of marriage and during the early childbearing years when she
was a member of an extended family household under the authority
of both older men and women. The status of a Haida woman was
highest when she occupied a specialist role such as shaman; when
she contributed property to and participated in her husband's
potlatches or hosted other types of potlatches on her own; when she
performed ritual acts as a father's sister (sqaʔan); and when, as a
widow, she remarried her husband's nephew over whom she had
virtually complete control. Though aboriginal Haida women
occupied a relatively high overall status as demonstrated in their
access to numerous domains of the culture, Haida society was
still a male dominated one. Men were the final authorities of the
household and the holders of positions of political authority. They

alone were the hosts of the most important types of potlatches, the owners of the most important property (houses and totem poles), the performers of the most prestigious rituals (dances), the creators and monopolizers of an art form whose symbols represented the matrilineal groups they dominated.

Acculturation both enhanced and undermined the status of women. Their position was strengthened at times when new economic opportunities were opened to them (potato cultivation and, later, perhaps prostitution) and when certain changes were effected in the social order (the creation of a women's interest group under missionization and changes in marriage practices). Demographic changes facilitated the entry of women into positions that were formerly male prerogatives, and women's greater leadership roles in potlatching and feasting derived in part from those same changes. The increasingly active role of women in the ceremonial complex was also encouraged by material changes, which (1) gave women the means (through the inheritance of husbands' estates) with which to host potlatches and feasts, and (2) identified the symbols of feasting as women's property.

The status of women was detrimentally affected by other acculturative processes. The Indian Act, a product of a patriarchal Victorian society, undermined traditional hereditary authority and effectively placed all decision-making in the hands of an elected male council. Criteria for Indian band membership, defined by the Act, made women's legal status much less secure (Mitchell 1976:172). The same acculturative philosophy that created the Indian Act deemed the public acknowledgment of women's natural reproductive functions shameful, and while this marked an end to pollution taboos and possibly to certain antagonisms between males and females, it also meant an end to the natural power that women enjoyed and the special public recognition of their femaleness.

The status of older women, always high, was both intentionally and unintentionally elevated with acculturation. Abolishment of the levirate and securement of the inheritance rights of widows gave these women the basic economic means to be full participants in the ceremonial culture. Their ceremonial and symbolic status has become increasingly important in the present day, as by virtue of age and survivorship they have become the final repositories of the native language, of ceremonial etiquette, of kinship, and of a heritage fast disappearing in the latter part of the twentieth century. Florence Davidson, respected and admired in her own community and by all outside of it who know her, is one of the last legatees.

CHAPTER 3

Florence Edenshaw Davidson:
A Biographical Sketch

The village of Masset was virtually deserted on the morning of September 15, 1896, when Florence Edenshaw was born in her father's house. Her "grandmother," Amy Edenshaw, who assisted at the birth, and her mother, Isabella, were among the few villagers who remained behind when the Masset people departed for the Ain River dog salmon fishery in early September.

Charles and Isabella Edenshaw already had two older daughters, Emily (Wałał gidák), sixteen years of age, and Agnes (Kwənt qayngás), eight.[1] Three other daughters, born in 1885, 1886, and 1891, had died in infancy.[2] Only a month before Florence's birth, Robert (Gináwən), the eldest son and a promising carver, had drowned at Rivers Inlet cannery. A second son, Albert Edward (Gusáwak), born in 1889, died at nine months of age. The family was eager for another son, but their disappointment was assuaged when the birth went without incident and the infant girl was healthy. Charles Edenshaw named his new daughter Jadał q'egəngá ("Story Maid"); her maternal uncle, Henry Edenshaw, who selected all the children's Christian names, called her Florence. Charles and Isabella had converted to Christianity and been baptized in the Anglican Church at Masset several years before, and so, on

1. Agnes' name describes a beached whale so large that all of it could not be used. Emily's name means "lots of things for the potlatch."
2. Florence only knew about the brothers who had preceded her. The female births were discovered in missionary records.

November 15, 1896, they took the infant Florence to be christened by the missionary. Prior to her baptism, Florence underwent a traditional Haida ritual: when four days old, her grandmother pierced her ears.

Charles Edenshaw adored his new daughter. "My Dad used to favor me," Nani says of their relationship. This was perhaps in part because she was believed to be the reincarnation of his own mother Qawkúna. "*Hada, ding awu di ijing*" ("Dad, I'm your mother") were Florence's first spoken words.[3]

Florence Davidson comes from a long line of distinguished Haida people (see genealogy). Her father was Chief Idínsaw, hereditary chief of the populous and powerful *Sdəłdás* Eagle lineage. He also bore the Haida names of Skił'wxan jas ("Fairies coming to you as in a big wave"), Dahʔégin ("Noise in the housepit"), the name bestowed in 1970 on the new elementary school at New Masset, and Nəngkwigetkłałs ("They gave ten potlatches for him"), conferred at his parents' final potlatch. The name Charles Edenshaw has become legendary in Northwest Coast art circles and his work has been the subject of intense scrutiny by scholars (see, for example, Barbeau 1944; Appleton 1970; Holm 1981). During his long and prolific artistic career from 1853 when he was fourteen years of age until a few years before his death in 1920, he produced scores of painted bentwood boxes, rattles, masks, miniature and large cedar totem poles, carved chief's staffs, argillite totem poles and sculptures, and gold and silver jewelry.

Though working within the confines of a longstanding Haida art tradition, Charles Edenshaw's work is distinctive and he is credited with several innovations, among them the introduction of carved gold and silver bracelets to the Haida. Edenshaw produced art for native use, including major works commissioned by natives of other tribes as well as jewelry purchased by local Haida at Masset and Skidegate on the Queen Charlotte Islands. He also carved for his family, making earrings and brooches for his young daughters out of the filings left from commissioned bracelets, and he fashioned a cedar chief's seat with his wife's crests (dogfish, grizzly bear, and killerwhale), which served as a divan in the family home during Florence's childhood.

Much of Charles Edenshaw's work, however, was commissioned by collectors for major museums whose orders kept the artist busy year-round. Dr. C. F. Newcombe, who collected for the Provincial

---

3. Traditionally, reincarnation was within the moiety if not the lineage. In this instance it was cross-moiety.

Museum in Victoria and Chicago's Field Museum, regularly purchased pieces from Edenshaw; Franz Boas bought some of Edenshaw's work at Port Essington in 1897 for the American Museum of Natural History in New York; John Swanton had Edenshaw carve numerous model totem poles and several model houses in 1901 to accompany his monograph on Haida culture; and, some of Edenshaw's last work was purchased by Masset Indian Agent Thomas Deasy, who later sold his entire collection to a wealthy eastern U.S. buyer.

Born at Skidegate in 1839, Charles Edenshaw was the heir of another prominent artist who bore the title of Chief Idínsaw before him. This was Albert Edward Edenshaw, Charles's mother's brother. Born around the year 1812, the elder Edenshaw had a reputation among his own people for being somewhat bellicose and was both respected and feared by white visitors to the islands. An extremely wealthy and powerful chief, he was frequently contacted by whites to lead exploring parties around the islands. In 1852 he earned the gratitude of the Hudson's Bay Company when he rescued the captain and crew of the ship *Susan Sturgis*, which had been looted and burned by a party under the leadership of Chief Weah, town chief at Masset. Edenshaw had houses at the northern Haida villages of Hiellen, Kung, and at Kiusta (see map) where he was town chief, but by the early 1880s, along with Haida from other outlying northern settlements, he moved to Masset.

Isabella Edenshaw (K'woiyəng) and her mother's sister Amy Edenshaw (Sɨnlágutgang) were members of the Shark House (*Q'ad nas*) *Y'akwə'lanas* Raven lineage originally of Klinkwan, Alaska. This lineage shows a long history of intermarriage with the *Sdəɬdás* lineage from the Queen Charlotte Islands, and Isabella and Amy in time followed the tradition. Isabella's mother, Ilsgide, for example, was married to Albert Edward Edenshaw's younger brother, and Amy's mother was married to a "brother" (lineage mate and perhaps actual brother) of Albert Edward Edenshaw's mother (see genealogy).

In the spring of 1862, Isabella, her Aunt Amy, and Wiba, a slave girl adopted as a playmate for Isabella who was an only child, were enroute home from Masset with their parents and a party of Kiusta Haida when the smallpox epidemic reached the Queen Charlottes. The two canoeloads of people had camped at Jalun River for the night, but by early morning when they were to depart for Kiusta, everyone but the three young girls had fallen ill with smallpox. Two *Y'akwə'lanas* uncles from Klinkwan who passed by Jalun River on their way home from Masset were able to rescue only Amy and Isabella. Wiba and the others at the camp perished with the disease.

Three or four years later when Amy reached marriageable age, she was taken by Albert Edward Edenshaw as his second wife. At the same time, the orphaned Isabella was fetched from Klinkwan and adopted by Edenshaw as his daughter. Albert and Amy Edenshaw had only one child, Henry, Florence Davidson's maternal uncle who is frequently mentioned in her narrative. Albert Edward Edenshaw died in 1894 and Amy was married in accordance with Haida tradition to his young lineage nephew, Phillip White, who looked after the aging lady until her death in 1922. Around 1873, Isabella Edenshaw was wed to Charles Edenshaw in a traditional Haida ceremony, and later, on December 27, 1885, following their conversion to Christianity, they were married in an Anglican service at St. Johns Church in Masset.

Charles Edenshaw inherited a traditional plank house from his uncle, but along with other Masset Haida, he soon built a Victorian-style cottage for his family.[4] Only the large grizzly bear mortuary pole honoring Isabella's mother's mother's sister, which stood in the front yard, bespoke the Haida affiliations of the new house's occupants.

The Edenshaws, like other Masset Haida of the time, moved about fairly frequently, remaining in Masset only during the late fall and winter months. For Florence and the other Masset children, wintertime meant school and Sunday school. Charlie Edenshaw spent the short winter days in his carving shed adjoining the house, and Isabella, having put up the family's winter supply of food, devoted her spare time to weaving the spruce root hats and baskets she would sell the following summer. She turned many of the completed hats and baskets over to her husband, who painted Haida designs on them. Florence often followed her father to his carving shed, accompanying him not so much because she admired his consummate skill as a carver, but because he always began his workday with prayer and she liked the way he prayed. Throughout the winter months there were "doings" of various kinds held in Masset: church gatherings, feasts, weddings, mortuary potlatches, welcome dances (*s'aⱴgá*), and a masked dance performance called *ƚiyá*, which Florence recalls seeing as a small child.

During her childhood years, Florence accompanied her parents at the end of February to Kung, the site of an old village in Naden Harbour; there they camped for a month or more to dry halibut. Returning only briefly to Masset, at the beginning of April (*t'aawkanut*,

4. Florence is not certain but thinks that all of her older siblings were born after Charles and Isabella moved into this white-style house.

Charles Edenshaw's house, c. 1900 (courtesy, British Columbia Provincial Museum)

or "gardening time") they left for Yatz, a former seal hunters' camp where the Haida now cultivated potato gardens. Here the men fished for halibut (except Charlie Edenshaw who continued to carve), while the women planted their gardens. From Yatz, the Edenshaws returned again to Masset. Early May brought the women and children briefly back to Yatz where they picked and dried seaweed. During much of May, though, the Edenshaws resided in Masset, and Florence accompanied her mother on frequent treks to North Beach to gather and process the spruce roots for Isabella's weaving. In June the Edenshaw family often left Masset on the steamer *Prince John* for the mainland. Isabella sold her baskets and hats at George Cunningham's store in Port Essington and there purchased yard goods for the family's winter wardrobe. Charles Edenshaw took his carving tools with him and continued to carve while his wife worked at Inverness Cannery on the Skeena River.

Some summers the Edenshaws went instead to Alaska and Isabella worked at the cannery in New Kasaan. In 1902 C. F. Newcombe visited them there, purchasing a spruce root cradle-liner painted with a dogfish design and some baskets from Isabella Edenshaw. He commissioned several items from Charles Edenshaw for the Field Museum and paid him twenty-five cents an hour for ethnographic information. That summer at the Kasaan cannery, Isabella gave birth to her last child, Alice (Skil Jade). Florence spent that and the next few summers looking after baby Alice and Nora, a sister three years Florence's junior.

When the family returned in late summer to the islands, Isabella and Florence picked huckleberries, crabapples, and salal berries. Late in the fall they gathered cranberries, and Isabella harvested her potatoes. The Edenshaws purchased or traded for their fall salmon; not until she was an adult did Florence go upriver to the Ain and Yakoun fish camps to slice, smoke, and later can, dog salmon and sockeye.

Florence attended the mission school at Masset until the fourth level, but her parents often needed her to help at home or to assist her Uncle Henry's wife, Martha, so attendance at school was sporadic. Still there was time for play and she recalls games with her Edenshaw cousins and friends Emma Matthews and Sophie Marks.

Childhood ended abruptly and unhappily for Florence with first her puberty seclusion, *təgwəná*, and then her arranged marriage to Robert Davidson, a respected and high-ranking man of the *C'ał'lanas* Eagle lineage more than twice her age. Envious as a child of the older girls who were whisked from their playmates at menarche and made to lie in a back room of the house for ten days or more, Florence, knowing nothing of menstruation, was frightened when it happened to her. A year and a half later she was not yet fifteen and still attending school when a party of *C'aƚ'lanas* and *Stl'əng'lanas* relatives of Robert Davidson's (the latter from his father's side) appeared at Charles Edenshaw's doorstep to propose the marriage of his daughter. "They were all streaming in and I don't know what's going on so I went to my uncle's house." A few days later she learned from an older cousin that she was about to be married. Horror struck, she defiantly told her mother that she would not marry "that old man" and she tearfully threatened to run away if they followed through with the wedding. "I wish I was dead," she remarked of her feelings when the wedding plans were formalized. The ensuing years eased the pain and in retrospect she speaks fondly of her husband, but she never forgot the bitterness she felt at being dragged from the side of her childhood friends into unsolicited wedlock.

Following their marriage on February 23, 1911, Robert and Florence Davidson moved in with Charles and Isabella Edenshaw. Not until two children were born did they move into a small home of their own. Alfred, the first of thirteen children, was born one year and ten months after their wedding. In succession followed Arnold (1914), Helen (1916), Virginia (1919), Reggie (1921), Joyce (1922), Claude (1924), Primrose (1926), Emily (1930), Myrtle (1931), Aggie (1933), Merle (1935), and Clara (1938). Spaced eighteen to thirty-one months apart, the children, Nani commented, were "just like stairsteps." Several of her children she delivered herself at home, though with some she had the assistance of her mother and elder sister Emily.

Four of the thirteen children died: Joyce at age three in 1925 at Ain River fish camp; Helen at eleven in 1928, Arnold at eighteen in 1933, and Reggie at thirty-seven in 1958. Today, seven of Robert and Florence Davidson's children live on the Queen Charlotte Islands: Aggie, Claude, Primrose, and Alfred in Haida Masset, and Virginia, Emily, and Merle in New Masset. Myrtle lives in Quesnel, and Clara, in Vancouver, British Columbia.

Childrearing was virtually a full-time job when the children were small. Nani lamented that while she had learned to read and write in school she had no time for either after she had young children to care for, and once she remarked that she wished she had learned all the stories and songs her husband knew. "There was no time; I always had a bunch of kids to look after." Nonetheless, she did

become an active member in the Anglican Church, joining the choir
and the Women's Auxiliary, and she worked to earn extra money for
her growing family. She baked bread and pastries at North Island to
sell to commercial fishermen; she labored summers in the canneries
at Masset, Naden, Tow Hill, and Rose Inlet; and, for a number of
years, she operated a small restaurant out of her home. Like her
mother before her she put up food for the family's winter use. She
gathered berries for jam and dried seaweed. In the fall she and her
husband fished for dog salmon at Ain River and in later years they
built a smokehouse and cabin on the Indian reserve at the mouth of
the Yakoun River where they fished for sockeye in late May and
early June. "I'm still working yet," Nani laughs, and indeed, in her
ninth decade she goes upriver for the sockeye salmon run, cooks for
feasts, and takes in boarders on a regular basis.

Robert Davidson was a commercial fisherman, but he also ran
a trapline in the Yakoun valley and for a time he worked as a
handlogger. As a young boy, he learned carpentry skills which
served him well throughout his life. He helped construct several
Masset houses, including his own, built fishing boats, and was
among the skilled Haida carpenters who in 1919 built the present
Anglican Church. Twice he rehoned old skills to build, with his
brother Alfred, traditional Haida canoes. No longer in use by
the Haida in 1909 when the first was built, the canoes were
commissioned by museums. In his declining years Robert took
up argillite carving, a skill he had learned years before from his
father-in-law, Charles Edenshaw.

In 1929 the Davidsons moved from their small cottage into a new
large two-story house designed and built by Robert. So ambitious
did some villagers think Robert Davidson's plans for the house that
they quipped, "Gəniyá [Robert] must be building a cannery." The
Davidsons celebrated the move with a feast, and two elders named
the house (*Naʔa q'Enadas*, "it's like summertime inside"; *Ne gut k'i
was*, "the main road runs by the house"). In 1952 the house was
destroyed in a fire and the Davidsons escaped with little more than
the clothes they were wearing. The laborious process of rebuilding
began, and two years later the family moved into the present
spacious one-story home. Robert Davidson finally paid off the loan
on the house with several of his argillite carvings.

The new house witnessed many celebrations as the years passed:
winter feasts, the wedding celebrations of Aggie, Merle, Myrtle,
and Clara, the golden wedding anniversary of Florence and Robert,
and the wedding feasts for several grandchildren. There were sad

1. Kiłgúlans married Qáwida upon Gináwən's death, as was the practice under the levirate.

2. Albert Edenshaw had two older brothers and three sisters, not shown here. Gə?wu aw was Albert Edenshaw's mother's brother's widow. Edenshaw married Amy while Gə?wu aw was still living.

3. Qawkúna married John Robson of Skidegate after K'łajangk'una's death.

4. Not all the offspring of these individuals are shown; furthermore, grandchildren's spouses and great-grandchildren are not shown on the genealogy.

Genealogy of Florence Edenshaw Davidson

KEY:

△	Male
○	Female
⌐⎯⌐	Marriage
│	Descendants
⌐⎯	Siblings
*	Mentioned in text
¦	Adopted

LINEAGE AFFILIATION:

Raven Moiety	Eagle Moiety	Non-Haida
△ Y'akwə'lanas	△ C'aɫ'lanas	△
△ Nikwən qiwe	△ Git?áns	
△ Stl'əng'lanas	△ Sdəɫdás	
△ Kwən'lanas		

5. Phillip White married Amy Edenshaw after the death of Albert Edenshaw.

6. Charles Edenshaw had three sisters, according to Florence Davidson.

7. Robert Davidson was a widower when he married Florence.

8. Florence's sisters, Nora and Agnes, both remarried later in life after they were widowed. Their second husbands, Robert Cogo and George Jones, are not shown on the genealogy.

celebrations in the large front room, too: memorial feasts and headstone raisings (mortuary potlatches) honoring deceased relatives.

Robert Davidson lived to see his namesake and grandson carve the first totem pole on the islands erected in the twentieth century; he died only a month later in September 1969, at the age of eighty-nine. Disconsolate for many months after her husband's death, Nani seldom left the house, but finally at the encouragement of the minister, she began taking in boarders. In short order there was a steady stream of teachers, nurses, visiting doctors and dentists, tourists, and researchers who stayed and enjoyed the comforts of her home and her Haida-Canadian cooking. Their names now fill Nani's several guest books and their enthusiastic comments express their warm regard for her.

CHAPTER 4

Those Before Me
(1862–1896)

The Northern Indians will be sent from the Reserve today to one of the islands in the Straits—there to rot and die with the loathsome disease which is now destroying the poor wretches at the rate of six each day. [*British Colonist*, May 13, 1862]

Forty out of sixty Hydahs who left Victoria for the North about one month ago, had died. The sick and dead with their canoes, blankets, guns, etc., were left along the coast. In one encampment, about twelve miles above Nanaimo, Capt. Osgood counted twelve dead Indians—the bodies festering in the noonday sun. [*British Colonist*, June 21, 1862]

They say a man saw the smallpox long before it happened. This man had a tent way before the white man came; my dad used to say he didn't know where the tent came from. The man was in his tent and someone who came near it said it smelled like perfume there. Something took the man up in the air; he must have dreamt he was in the air above all the island. He saw all the villages, but they were torn up and they looked empty. Just Masset and Skidegate were all right. The ones who took the man up told him just two villages would be left and the rest would be wiped out because the people were getting too bad. Two men would be leaders of these villages, they said. They meant Alfred Adams and Peter Kelly.

Smallpox came from Victoria. On the way home where the people camped overnight, some would get sick and they'd leave the sick ones there. It spread all over the islands. Both of my mother's parents died in the smallpox epidemic and my grandmother's parents, too. They were going home to Kiusta from Masset. My mother's parents were on one canoe, my grandmother's on the other. There were some other people from Kiusta with them. They stayed overnight at Jalun River and put up cedar-bark tents. They were supposed to leave right away the next morning but they took sick. They all got sick at once. My mother's mother, Ílsgide, was a young woman with just one child, a four-year-old girl, my mother. Ílsgide was married to Albert Edward Edenshaw's younger brother; I don't even know his name. When Ílsgide took sick, she went into the water up to her chest. Then she went back to the lean-to where they had built a big fire. She went underneath her blanket and right away she went to sleep and died.

My "grandmother," Amy, was about ten years old then. She was really Ílsgide's sister, but ever since I can remember my mother never told us Amy was her aunt; we used to think Amy was her mother. Amy and my mother and Wiba, my mother's playmate, were the only ones who didn't take sick. My mother's parents bought a playmate for my mother because she's alone, the only child. Wiba's parents were slaves, but my mother's parents bought her so my mother would have someone to play with; they didn't buy her for a slave. They were going to adopt her. The little girls were playing on the beach when their uncles, Gináwən and Kiłgúlans, came by from Masset on their way to Klinkwan [Alaska]. Amy's father saw the canoe landing and told them not to stop because they were all sick; he didn't want them to catch smallpox. The uncles grabbed the two little girls, my mother and Amy. Wiba was a little ways from them, and they couldn't get to her because my grandmother's father had a gun. He was shooting at them, trying to kill them because they took the two girls. When my mother talked about Wiba she used to cry. Wiba ran after them but they couldn't rescue her because Amy's father had the gun. She got left there and she wasn't even sick. I guess she died with the rest. They were all wiped out; no one was saved from there. My grandmother used to tell me the story of it when I was little.

My "Grandfather": Albert Edward Edenshaw

This worthy Haida Chief died at Masset November 16, 1894. He was a great friend of mine and one for whom I had greatest respect. He practically did his utmost to promote a feeling of good fellowship between the whites and the Haidas. . . . From the first day of my arrival I had his support and influence, and it was through his untiring energy that the Haidas finally cast off heathenism. . . . He did not receive [the] name [Edenshaw] at his birth, but when he succeeded his uncle as the chief of the Shongalth Lennas[1], who had their headquarters at Dadens, near North Island. His birth name was Gwai-gu-unlthin, which means according to a recent interpretation, the man who rests his head on an island. The village in which he was born had disappeared, but if reports be true it was situated near Cape Ball on the eastern shore of Graham Island about 40 to 45 miles from Skidegate. . . . Edenshaw was an old man when I first met him, and I should have judged him to be about 70 years old. If this were correct it would give the year of his birth about 1812.

His early youth was spent during the time the Haidas were at the zenith of their power. . . . He has often told me of the many wars against the Zimshians and the Naass Indians[2] that he had been engaged in and how victorious he and his party always were. . . . Edenshaw had two brothers older than himself, and they were considered to be very brave men, and young Edenshaw did his utmost to be considered as brave as they were. . . . He made Skidegate, I think, his home until he was appointed chief. . . . The uncle he succeeded was a most powerful chief at Dadens near Cape Knox, and bore the hereditary name of Edinso. . . . A few years prior to his being called to prepare for the chieftainship his two eldest brothers had died. According to Haida descent he had to marry the chief's, i.e. his uncle's daughter, but his uncle had no daughter in his family, consequently it was arranged that he should marry a daughter of an excellent and powerful chief in Alaska. His uncle finally died and Edenshaw succeeded to his property and chieftainship, and at his succession the grandest and largest distribution of goods and articles of great value including slaves took place that has ever been known on these islands. [Harrison, August 26, 1912]

Young Chief Edenshaw's property included 12 slaves, male and female, and when he became united to his wife, his wife's father gave his daughter 10 more slaves to take with her to her new home. . . . [Harrison, September 2, 1912] Edenshaw's friends say that he never captured slaves himself, though he constantly bought and sold them. He obtained them chiefly from Skidegate and often went as far as Sitka to sell them. He used to travel in state in a dugout canoe twelve fathoms long, elaborately painted at both ends, manned by a large number of slaves and dependents. By means of constant trading he accumulated a large quantity of property, and in the course of his life made no less than seven large potlatches. [Harrison, September 16, 1912]

When [the Hudson's Bay] company had their store opened at

1. Or, *Sdałdás*, Swanton's E 21 (1909:275).
2. Tsimshian and Nass (River) Indians. The latter are usually referred to as the Nishga.

Massett, Edenshaw and his followers were amongst the first to come
together and form one united settlement of the Northern Haidas at
Massett. I had the privilege of baptising him and his wife and of
receiving them into the church. They were afterwards confirmed by
Bishop Ridley and became communicants. When baptised he received
the name Albert Edward, the Christian name of the late King Edward.
[Edenshaw's] eldest son, George Cowhoe, was the first native teacher
on these Islands, and I also had the privilege of baptising him, his wife,
and family. He [Edenshaw] had only two sons and the other is so well
known that he needs no recommendation from me. His name is Henry
Edenshaw. I baptised him also. After his brother's death he succeeded
him in his chieftainship and also became the teacher of the Masset
Indian school, which position he filled remarkably well for several
years. He is now franchised and entitled to all the privileges of the
white man, and no better business man can be met with on this entire
coast . . . .

   I have no hesitation in saying that it is principally due to his
[Edenshaw's] manlike ways, his influence, and example that the Haidas
have taken so readily to the ways and customs of the whites, and that
at the present moment they are one of the most advanced and law-
abiding races on the coast. [Harrison, October 21, 1912]

My grandmother didn't tell me about my grandfather; I didn't
even know till much later that he was the chief.
   After the smallpox Albert Edenshaw took his uncle's place. His
uncle at Kiusta sent for him; he was away at Port Simpson. That old
man must have been living yet while everyone else was wiped out
with smallpox. When the old man died, Albert Edward married his
wife. She was my grandmother's aunt [Amy's mother's sister]. They
lived at Kiusta and there Albert Edenshaw built a house with ten *day*
[steps down to the housepit].[3] In the mornings when the sun used
to come up his wife liked to sit at the front of the house with her
elbows on her knees and her face in her hands, enjoying the
sunshine. She had copper and gold bracelets from her wrists to her
elbows and copper ones even on her ankles. The sun made them
really shiny. She used to sit like that before the house because she
was so precious. They called her Gəʔwu aw, "Gəʔwu's mother."
Gəʔwu was her only son.[4] Gəʔwu aw was kind of old, older than her
husband, and it's hard for her that my mother and grandmother
were in Klinkwan with their uncles. The little girls were far away
from her that's why it's hard for her. Albert Edward wanted to go for

   3. The number "10," a ritual number in Haida, recurs throughout
Florence's narrative.
   4. Gəʔwu is the George Cowhoe (a corruption of the Haida "Gəʔwu")
referred to in Harrison's account.

Albert Edward Edenshaw, *far right*, 1890 (courtesy, Public Archives of Canada, C60824)

them and bring them to Kiusta, and Gəʔwu aw agreed with him that he should marry Amy, too.

Albert Edward didn't want Amy and my mother to be poor, so when Amy was old enough to marry, my grandfather went to get her on a canoe with ten slaves to paddle for him. He took the girls from Klinkwan to Kung in Naden Harbour where he had a new house. There they had a wedding ceremony and for days and days they potlatched. Albert Edward potlatched for the girls because they were orphans. He married my grandmother and adopted my mother as his daughter. He had a big pole raising and watəł [potlatch] for the young girls. Maybe my grandmother's parents had potlatched for Amy, but my mother was too small yet. Her parents were still gathering things to potlatch when they died; they were just a young couple.

My mother was tattooed at the doing my grandfather held; she had a long dogfish on one leg, a grizzly bear on the other, and a quarter moon and lady on each arm.[5] The tattoos were done in red and blue. They tried to put a tattoo on her chest but she didn't want it and wouldn't let them do it. Maggie Yeltatzie [Florence's sister's husband's sister] was one of the last people tattooed. She was real ashamed of the tattoos on her hands. She used to wear gloves to hide them whenever she went out. "I wonder why I let them do this to me," she used to say.

Albert Edward Edenshaw had houses in several villages besides Kiusta and they kept moving around. His house at Kiusta with ten *day* was the biggest house, they say. He was a sea otter hunter and he used to hang the furs up at the back of the house, *t'əcgwa*, the chief's place. My mother used to like to lie by the furs and run her hands over them and blow on them. They were so nice, just like silk, she said.

Amy and my grandfather had one child, Henry Edenshaw. When he was born, my grandfather's other wife, Gəʔwu aw, used to look after him real good. When Henry was old enough to get married, he had a girlfriend here in Masset, but she wasn't near enough [in terms of kinship]. My grandmother wanted him to marry Martha Duncan because that was her uncle's daughter, and he did.

My Parents

My mother and Emma Matthews' mother used to play together at Kiusta. They're related; their mothers were cousins. My grandfather

5. Isabella's tattoos are depicted in Swanton (1909:Pl. XXI).

had never seen a doll before but he used to make dolls for my
mother. Near Kiusta there's a cave with stalactites and stalagmites
growing in it. They used to believe it was a "ghost house"; if you
couldn't get babies you and your husband go in there and you start
getting babies after that. My grandfather took the stalactites and
carved the face and arms and legs on them. He collected hair from
my mother's comb and he glued it on the doll's head. My mother
said she used to wash the doll's hair all the time when she was little.

Emma's mother and my mother used to play on a *t'aawʔk'a* a lot.
It's a big dugout dish they put steamed food in to cool off before
serving. I never saw one; they didn't use them during my time.
They made a little paddle for the girls so they could paddle around
in the water on the *t'aawʔk'a*. One slave sat on each side of the
dugout to watch over them. They were ready to jump in and grab
the little girls right away in case they tipped over.

My mother's name was K'woiyəng. "K'woiyəng," I wonder what
it means? She was named after her *nanləng* who belonged to
Kwən'lanas.[6] She had her own name too; I think it was S'it kwuns,
"Red Moon." She got the name Isabella just before she and my dad
were married in the church. My mother had light brown hair and
real white skin and gray eyes. Her mother and her uncles were like
that too. Gináwən, her uncle, had light curly hair and big blue eyes.
My grandmother Amy was the same. That was because they came
from a woman who was married, in the Indian way, to a white boat
captain. Wintertime he took his wife and children down south to
Victoria, but summertime his wife was lonely for her relatives in
Klinkwan and Kiusta, so he took her home every summer. The
lady's name was Ninasɨnlahelawas. She had about five children from
that captain. My mother was so light-skinned that after she married
my dad and went to Skidegate, my dad's auntie and his parents got
medicine for her. They were afraid she was going to have a short life
because she was so white, so they made her take Indian medicine. I
used to have a picture of my mother when she was a young woman.
The picture was taken in Victoria. She's standing with a fern beside
her and she looks just like a white lady. The picture was on tin.

My dad's father, K'łajangk'una, belonged to *Nikwən qiwe*;
Qawkúna, his wife, was *Sdəłdás*.[7] K'łajangk'una was a real good
carver and canoe builder from Skidegate. Qawkúna used to go with
her husband when he cut trees for canoes. She had lots of names,

6. *Nanləng* (or "grandmothers") are women of father's father's lineage.
7. Swanton's R 13 and E 21, respectively (1909:270, 275).

but I only know one other one—Itɬgujatgut'aas. It means a rich woman grabs heavy things with her claws like an eagle.

Qawkúna and her husband used to take Indian medicine all the time. Once she went out with her husband and they found a *s'it* [cryptochiton] at the bottom of a tree. That's a lucky sign, so she took it. If you come across anything from the sea in the woods, it's a lucky sign. You eat it for luck and you keep the shells in a bentwood box. After that it's easy to get anything; you become richer and richer. My grandfather, Albert Edward, once found a lucky sign, too. He was going up into the woods: it wasn't summertime yet but the bluebottles were clustered on some halibut gills, *haagu c'an*. They were moving, just like a killerwhale sounding. *Kwaagíndal*, they call it. Amongst the moss it went. Albert Edward grabbed it and he became *skíɬíɬdá*, "lucky." [8]

When my dad was first born they gave him the name Dahʔégin ["noise in the housepit"]. While he was growing up his parents potlatched for him ten times. He had lots of names; the last one he got—Nəngkwigetklaɬs—means "they gave ten potlatches for him." When he was little his parents thought he was so precious that when he was sleeping they left the longhouse door open so they don't make any noise going in and out. They had a stick to push the door up so he won't wake up.

My dad was tattooed at his parents' potlatches. He had no clean skin he was so tattooed. Even his back, his arms, his legs, his chest, his hands were tattooed. I don't remember all the crests he's got tattooed, just eagle, sea wolf, and frog. My grandmother [Amy Edenshaw] thought my dad wasn't healthy because he's got so many tattoos on his body. She used to call him *"paysen"*; she meant "poison," germy.

> There was also a native jeweller in each village who made from half dollar and dollar silver coins, and also from gold coins, bracelets, bangles, finger rings and earrings. The first man to attempt the manipulation of the silver and gold was chief Edenshaw. [Harrison, May 27, 1912]

8. Other examples of lucky signs mentioned by Florence include frog nests, hummingbird nests, and owl skins (taken from an owl that has landed on one's head). If one ignores a lucky sign and does not take the object home, it is believed that misfortune will follow and one will have a short life. Swanton (1909:30) describes a creature similar to the halibut gills found by Albert Edenshaw.

Masset lay readers, c. 1910. *Left to right, seated:* Richard Russ, Charles Edenshaw, Rev. William E. Collison, James Stanley, Thomas Weir; *standing:* Sam Davis, Henry Edenshaw, Robert Ridley, Frederick Young (courtesy, Provincial Archives of British Columbia)

My father started carving one winter when he was sick. When he was about fourteen he was sick all winter long. He was in bed, but he got some argillite and started carving a totem pole. He was so sick he didn't want to eat anything, but his mother had an iron pot and she put hot water, seaweed, and grease in it, and she made my dad eat it. In May he got better. He took a walk and something came out from his chest right up his throat. He spit it in the creek. It looked like a devilfish with legs on it. That's what made him sick, and as soon as he got rid of it he got better. After that he carved his first bracelet, out of five silver-dollar pieces melted together. Later, after he married my mother but before my time, he used to go to Victoria and carve all winter long.

Maybe my dad was about eighteen or nineteen when he came to Masset. His uncle, Albert Edward Edenshaw, wanted him, so he came here. And when it was time, he married my mother. They were married in the Indian way before the missionaries came.

When Mr. Harrison [Rev. Charles Harrison, missionary] came here, he married my parents in the church. Just before they got married, Mr. Harrison baptized them. My mother didn't read so Mr. Harrison mentioned lots of names to her. When he said "Isabella," she said "yes." He told her it was a queen's name; that's why she likes it, I guess. Albert Edward put my dad in his [Albert Edward's] place while he was still living. When my dad married my mother in the church that's when his uncle gave him the name Edenshaw. When the missionary called my mother Isabella Edenshaw, she wouldn't take the "Edenshaw" for a long time. She couldn't understand it; "How can I take Eagle's name?" she kept asking. Finally she gave up.

A lady named Kwoiyat gudang awu ["Kwoiyat's mother"] willed my dad a longhouse in Masset after her husband died. Her husband was my dad's tribe [lineage], one of his uncles. That was the time that my dad gave a big potlatch for his two children, Emily and Gináwən, my older sister and brother. By the time my parents had Agnes, they moved to a white man's [style] house. My mother had another boy, born before me. His name was Gusáwak, Albert Edward. His neck swelled up and he died when he was nine months old. My parents lost the only boys in the family.

CHAPTER 5

Before I Could Walk
(1896–1897)

What I think would most forcibly strike a stranger visiting our village for the first time is its civilized aspect. A formidable line of totem poles running along the main street still indeed proclaims the place an Indian settlement: but the Indian lodges which once stood behind each of these poles have almost disappeared and shapely wooden cottages—all built by the natives themselves—have taken their place. At the back of almost every house is a garden where the owner grows sufficient potatoes to supply his wants. A few of the Indians also keep horses and cows.

The interior of the houses, it must be confessed, are not yet what one would wish to see them. The habits of the lodge are still in several cases retained. . . . However, things are improving and many of the younger people now take their meals at tables and sleep on bedsteads instead of passing their existence like their forefathers on the floor. [Keen 1894]

When I was on the way [summer 1896], my mother and dad and the whole family—Gináwən [Robert], Emily, Agnes—went to Juneau, Alaska. It was springtime and they went by canoe. My brother had the navigation chart and he used to tell dad how they're going to come across a camp or something. They'd stay at the camp overnight and start again to Juneau. My brother would look at the chart and say, "we're going to come across an iceberg tomorrow," and my dad would be real surprised when he saw it.

My dad went to Alaska to carve. Gináwən was a carver, too, and my dad used to say that his son's work was the best of all. When they finished working, they sold the canoe and they took the steamer, c'an ƛuwe [sea canoe], to Victoria. My mother wanted a treadle sewing machine. My dad said, "We'll go down to Victoria to buy it," and the whole family went to Victoria to buy this treadle machine. They bought a lot of things there. On the way back the steamer stopped at Rivers Inlet where most of the Masset people were working in the cannery. My grandmother [Amy Edenshaw] and my step-grandfather [Phillip White] were there. Gináwən used to love his grandmother and she used to love him so much. "I'm going to stay with my grandmother," he told his parents. "I'll come home with them when they're through working."

When they were done working in the cannery and almost ready to go home, Gináwən went out swimming. He dived in and didn't come up for a long time. My husband, who was only twelve or thirteen then, watched him for a long time and got worried when he didn't come up. A good diver came around and he found Gináwən on the bottom, face down. They worked on him for a long time. Finally they quit and took the body home.

My grandmother had gone to the inlet where the stream was to wash clothes. She and Phillip were there and you could hear her laughing clear from the mouth of the bay when they came with the bad news. "Sɨnlagutgang!" They called her name real loud and she stopped laughing. "Something terrible happened. Your Gináwən drowned." Then they took my grandmother and her husband home, towing their little boat.

In those days when someone died at the cannery, the Chinamen would build the casket, nail the box up, and put a nice expensive cover on it. Sarah Brooks's brother [from Masset] died the same time as Gináwən, and there were two caskets on the steamer when the Masset people came home from Rivers Inlet.

My mother and dad were staying in a tent at Fort Simpson waiting for the steamer and their son. When the steamer was coming my mother started cooking and Emily and Agnes put nice dresses and summer hats on to meet their brother. But there's no Gináwən. My dad was coming, too, and he stopped halfway there, feeling that something happened to his son because nobody was getting off the boat. Finally, Agnes Williams' father walked up to my dad and just hugged him. "Kilsle [chief], something terrible happened to you." And he grabbed him because he knew my dad was going to jump off the wharf and drown himself. All the people around cried with my dad and tried to get him and the family on the boat to go across to Masset. My mother and grandmother ran and threw themselves in the water; it was so hard for them. They tried to stop them, and finally they got them on the steamer.

They came home in late August. My uncle, Henry Edenshaw, was

Masset in 1911

anxious for his nephew. He was going to cut hay across the inlet for his cows and when his wife Martha asked him when he was going to cut hay, he said, "I'm waiting for Gináwən; we'll work together." He made Martha put all kinds of food together to take across. When my parents and grandmother got home and told him the bad news he took it as hard as they did. He cried and no one could stop him.

I was born in September. People had gone up the inlet [Masset Inlet] to dry fish and pick berries; there were hardly any people here. All the people were wishing my mother would get a boy but I disappointed them. And I'm still living. When I was born my grandmother was real happy. Even though I was a girl she was happy because the trouble [labor] was over. When a baby is born the first mess it makes is black. They used to take this, get a stick, and paint eyebrows on with it. They did it so the baby's eyebrows don't point down. My grandmother made my eyebrows like that. She pierced my ears when I was four days old. The sqa ʔanləng[1] used to do it in the olden days, but my grandmother was so happy that I was born and that my mother was safe. They called me Jadał q'egəngá right away after my nanləng. My father gave me my Indian name and my uncle called me Florence. My mother and dad didn't read, that's why Henry Edenshaw gave all of us names. Mr. Keen, the missionary, baptized me.

I don't know the story of my name well. There was a young lady. They say she was a "princess" [y'aʔʕEyt, high ranking]. She came on a small canoe and drifted ashore at Rose Spit. A young man found her and asked her name. "Just holler 'jadał q'egnadła gEl go-oooo,' 'the story maid arrives,' and say 's'aan jat gu sandlan tla gEl go-oooo,' 'the killerwhale maid arrives.'"[2] He kept on hollering the names because she was y'aʔʕEyt and didn't want to come into shore quietly. She told the man to hide her underneath the canoe; she put it upside down and she used to lie underneath it. That's all I know; I don't know how they found out about her. She was Nikwən qiwe, my dad's father's tribe [lineage], the very first one. My name means "Story Maid"—that generations after, the story of that woman will be known. Because I got the name I hate it when they talk about it; it

---

1. Sqaʔanləng are women of father's matrilineage. The English term "auntie" is often given today as an equivalent.

2. The second name, according to Peter Kelly (Morley 1967:32), translates "Women on Whom the First Dawn Came." This woman was the ancestress of the Nikwən qiwe; no one knows where she came from. This second name was given to Nora, Florence's younger sister.

sounds awful to me because she drifted ashore and a man found her.

I don't know who had the name before me. Henry Young from Skidegate told me no one could be fit enough to be named after this *y'a ʔᵡEyt* girl; no one could be like her. "First time someone is named after her and you're the only one who fits it," he said to me.

After I was born, I used a cradle for about one year, I guess, and my sister Nora used the cradle after me. It was carved by my dad, with a dogfish on the bottom. In 1903 when my parents were in Victoria, they sold the cradle to Mr. Newcombe.[3]

3. The cradle is shown in color in N. Bancroft-Hunt's *People of the Totem* (1979:46 [New York: Orbis Publishing]).

CHAPTER 6

I Am Yet a Girl
(1897–1909)

I find it a good plan to stay long enough in a mission to thoroughly enter into the life of the people so as to be able to understand the conditions which prevail.

It is a pity though the people do not stay longer at a time in their village. All summer most of them are on the coast of the mainland working at the canneries . . . so it is from October to February that most of the work must be done among them here.

The last time there was confirmation in this church was when it was opened *eighteen* years ago.

Before long there may be a white settlement on Masset Inlet.

Sunday services are attended by 150–200 people (350 population). The morning service is in Haida—except the hymns and chants, and the evening service (as is the custom in the diocese) is in English. The young people all much prefer the English service. It is much better attended than the other. [Du Vernet 1906]

My mother said I was real fast in everything. I walked around real early and I started talking when I was small. My dad used to favor me because I used to tell him, *"Hada, ding awu di ijing,"* "Dad, I'm your mother."[1] They used to believe in second-birth [reincarnation]. *"Hada ding awu di ijing,"* I kept on saying. Those were my first words.

1. Favorite children are quite common among the Haida. Florence noted that Aggie was her husband's favorite child, but in regard to her own preferences said, "I love them all."

78

I don't remember when my sister Emily got married; I was too small, I guess. She must have been about fifteen when she married Henry White, and right after, Agnes got married.[2] They came for Agnes from Alaska. When there's no one to marry at home, chiefs' children marry someone from a different village. Agnes married Alec Yeltatzie from Howkan. They even cooked for the wedding at my dad's house, but I can't remember anything of it. I didn't know they were married but I remember when Carrie [Agnes' first child] was born. I remember Emily's first baby, too. When Emily had her first boy, Gusáwak, I said to my mother, "Why don't you call me by Emily's name, then I could be having a baby now, too." My mother laughed about it for a long time.

Ever since I can remember I'd go with my dad to watch him carve. Wintertime he used to work in the shed behind our house. When we were all grown up he started carving in the house. As soon as he finished breakfast he'd be ready to go out and I'd be ready to go with him. He sat on a little armchair with the legs cut off so it was low to the ground. He had a little box beside him where I used to sit. Soon as he sat down at his carving table, he'd take off his cap and he'd pray every morning. That's why I used to go out with him; I enjoyed his praying so much. When he was through, he'd start carving. I'd sit there for awhile and I'd say, "Dad, I'm going now," and he'd say, "Oh." Kindly, he said it.

My dad used to make little longhouses, and I used to want them real bad to play with, but I didn't tell him. He used to make all kinds of earrings for me. I would lose just one earring all the time and he'd make a new one. "Your dad will fix another earring for you because you look like a boy," my mother would say. She used to get kind of mad at me when I'd lose my earrings. My dad made just gold earrings for me, because I was his favorite, his mother's second birth.

My parents didn't own much of my dad's work. What they had they sold. My mother even sold her bracelets when people wanted them. We had a chesterfield in our house that my dad carved for my mother. It was like a chief's seat, with a *q'ad* [dogfish] on it and a *xudj* [grizzly bear]. It had *xudj* tracks on it—*st'asəl*, we call the tracks. My mother put a feather mattress on it and we used it for a

2. Emily married in 1900 at age twenty (Florence was four years old at the time). Agnes married in 1902. Information on both marriages comes from the St. John's Anglican Church marriage register.

Chief's seat carved by Charles Edenshaw (courtesy, Museum of the American Indian, Heye Foundation)

chesterfield. It went to Alec [Yeltatzie] when he took my dad's place, and he and Agnes sold it for $150 to buy a casket for their son who died.[3]

My dad used to get orders for things, poles and jewelry, and he would work on them all the time. When my mother went to work in the cannery my dad would stay home to work on his carving. When I was little we went to Ketchikan summers so my dad could carve and my mother work at the saltery there. When my dad finished his work he'd always tell me, "I'm going to sell my things," and I'd wash my hair and put clean clothes on. I'd get ready real quick and I wouldn't play around after so I could be clean when I went to town. The people would give him money for his work and we'd go to the grocery store. "Dad, can you give me five cents?" I would say. He always gave me a quarter. I bought a "prize" box, little candy box with a prize in it. I used to collect it for my friends. I gave the prizes to my friends but I ate the candy.

I liked going to the store. My mother used to buy all her woolen

3. The chief's seat is on display in the Museum of the American Indian in New York.

material in Ketchikan and she made our clothes from that. She bought coats for us from George Cunningham's store in Port Essington on the mainland. James Martin was the first one to have a store in New Masset, here on the islands. When my mother and dad and I would go up to New Masset on a row boat I thought I was going to a city. I just saw one store there but I enjoyed it very much.

When my parents went to Ketchikan I used to look after my youngest sister Alice while my mother worked at the cannery. My mother used to feed her with condensed milk. She had a big bottle with a long rubber tube to it. I gave Alice the milk, and soon as she was finished I filled the bottle up with milk for myself. I made it real strong and real hot so I could taste the rubber tube. I was sucking away at the bottle when my dad turned around from his carving and looked at me. "*Um-uh, um-uh,*" he said. He was surprised, that's what that means. My sister Nora was younger than me, but she was gentle. She never did anything crazy like that.

One time when my mother was working at the saltery in Ketchikan salting spring salmon, she told me to cook rice for her and have it ready when she got home. I took the bag of rice out to the tap to wash it, but instead of washing it I threw two handfuls on the walk. "Don't, don't do that, sister," Nora said. "I'm doing it so Mum will think it's snowing when she gets back." When my mother came in the door she said, "Why's there so much rice on the walk?" I didn't say anything, just pretended to be busy. Nora told her I did it. My mother told me not to do it again; she said they're going to call me crazy if I do it again, and I was real scared.

When we went to Inverness cannery summers I used to pick berries there. "I'm going to pick berries for my dad," I always said. I picked blueberries and salmonberries. When I came home from picking berries, Eliza Nałang, my husband's mother, would be going for water. "I'll go for your water," I said, and she would be real happy. I was about ten when she died and they had the doing at Masset to pay people who looked after the body.[4] Because I used to pack water for her they paid me. They asked my mother to bring me along to the doing. I was so proud; you know how little girls are. They don't invite kids my age and I was the only little girl there. They passed tobacco to the men to smoke and they gave out dishes,

4. Florence refers here to the mortuary potlatch given after the death of a person when the tombstone (formerly mortuary totem pole) is lifted into place. Members of the moiety opposite the deceased's perform the important mortuary rituals and are reimbursed for their services at the potlatch that follows.

blankets, and yard goods. The men got about five blankets, the small Hudson's Bay ones with black stripes. They gave me four fathoms of dress goods. They used to use Tommy Nutcome's house for doings because it had a big room. When I was young they passed soda pop [*ginálga hawla*, "something sweet"] around at doings. Strawberry, raspberry, any kind of berry flavor. Wintertime they would put it in big pots and one or two people packed it around. They scooped it up in a dipper and gave it to you to drink. When you gave the dipper back they'd get some for the next person. They didn't think about germs in those days.

About a year after that doing I started working in the cannery at Inverness. I was eleven. We piled empty cans in the trays. When we'd filled all the trays we left work. We'd go out for awhile and we'd forget to come back. We'd come back to work whenever we remembered it. I used to get five cents an hour, but I enjoyed that time.

When we came back to Masset from the cannery I used to pick berries with my mother. We went up to New Masset for salal. There weren't any white people there then, just all kinds of berries. My mother also used to go to Watun River for red huckleberries and I went with her. She'd bring the berries home and cook them with salmon eggs for thickening. She boiled them till they were dry. She put the berries in a bentwood box with a cloth covering over them, then thimbleberry leaves and skunk cabbage leaves on top before she put the lid on. She cooked her berries in the shed behind the house where my dad carved and she stored them there, too. She cooked salal berries the same way. My mother put up huckleberries, salal, and cranberries in boxes, five or six of them, for the winter. She used to jam blueberries in big jars and she preserved maltberries and crabapples in water. My dad had a little dugout [*qsotɬu*, "sea otter canoe"], and my mother, Emma Matthews' mother, and Alfred Adams' mother used to paddle out to Tow Hill to pick crabapples in October. I didn't go with them; I guess they didn't want to take me. They'd spend days and days there and get real lots of crabapples. Sometimes they'd pick the stems off and preserve the apples in a barrel. Other times they'd cook the apples, just simmer them, and put them in a barrel. Wintertime they'd take the juice out. It tastes like apple cider. Then they'd whip up grease and mix the apples with grease and sugar. *K'oi qayudiya*, they called it. They put the mixture in a bent box, put a clean flour sack on top, and put roasted thimbleberry leaves and roasted skunk cabbage leaves on top of that cloth. They packed clean sand on top of the leaves so air doesn't get in.

Falltime my parents didn't go with the other people up to Ain River to fish for salmon. We used to buy our salmon from other people. I didn't go to Ain River fish camp until after I was married.

Fall and winter I spent most of my time helping my uncle, Henry Edenshaw, and his wife. I liked working with Martha. My mother loved her brother [Henry] so much; she thinks highly of him, so I helped them. Young girls used to help their uncle's wife all the time. I was supposed to be going to school but my uncle's wife needed me, so instead of going to school I stayed home to wash diapers by Martha. I was staying by my uncle falltime when I was about eleven and he told me, "Florence, you get up early in the morning and cook porridge." So I got up around six o'clock to cook the porridge. First time I ever cooked porridge, so I was rushing around. I boiled water in the kettle and I took the big pot out and I put rolled oats in it. While the porridge was cooking I was real tired so I lay down in the kitchen and I went off to sleep. My uncle came in and said, "EH!" and I woke up. I got up to see the porridge and it was real hard. My, I was scared of my uncle. "Did you cook porridge before?" he asked me. "No." "Just your mother cooks it?" "Yes." "No wonder it's so good!" I don't remember if they ate it or not.

I used to stay home from school most of the time to help my uncle. Their house was kind of like a hotel—they had about eight rooms for guests. I looked after their dining room when white people used to stay there and I fixed the beds and cleaned up the rooms.

I was a handyman for my parents, too. I used to go out with my dad to get wood in the wintertime, just like a boy can do. Soon as I can pull a handsaw I'd go with him. I felt sorry for my dad; I didn't want him to go alone so we cut wood together.[5] I was a strong little girl, I guess. I used to pack the wood out with him to the boat. One time we went and I saw a bunch of snow there. "Dad," I said, "I'm going to take this home to eat it with milk." He said it's all right, so I took off my kerchief and put lots of snow in it. When I got home I got the chills and next day I caught pneumonia. I was sick for more than one month. I don't think my dad took me out after that to go for wood again.

Once when I was real small my dad went down past where the cemetery is to collect some driftwood. His dugout was too full, I guess, and he tipped over. Robert Williams' dad and Tl'aʔʕuntz, a [former] slave, saved him. Because they were the opposite tribe

5. A man was usually assisted by his nephews, but Charles Edenshaw had none in Masset.

[moiety] from my dad, there's a big doing. Ṣǝnsǝngáda, they call it. All the Eagle tribe gave money to my dad.[6] John Robson, my dad's stepfather, made a big paper eagle and they nailed it up on the wall. They paid Robert Williams' dad and Tl'aʔ꞉untz lots of money and they had a feast and Indian dancing. I was there but that's all I remember; it was just like a dream to me.

Wintertime when I was small they used to dance so much: The s'aꞡá,[7] they called the dances. They just did them for fun so they don't forget them. Some used to wear masks but after white people come around here they cleaned out all the masks. Too bad I didn't learn the songs. I used to see it in Tommy Nutcome's house; they used to dance there all the time. I remember when they used to dance kłiyá. Kłiyá wasn't part of the s'aꞡá. They used to go around the village saying, "We're going to see kłiyá tonight," and all the children would be real excited. The mask was real big and wide with a big nose and mouth. The eyes were red and behind the mouth was red. Little kids used to be really scared of it. I don't know what kłiyá means in English.[8]

In February we used to go to Gwǝs, near Kung. We stayed there for a long time until we got lots of halibut and dried it. We used to barbecue the halibut, the bony neck part. The tail and the head were boiled, to eat with seaweed.

April they call t'aawkanut, "gardening time." My grandparents [Amy and Phillip], my parents, my sisters, and I would go on a little canoe to Yatz to plant gardens. Lots of people from Masset went there to garden. They cut the eyes out of the potatoes to plant and we ate the middle part; they called that part scusid stłuʔEl, "potato's

6. Ṣǝnsǝngáda, which Murdock (1936) refers to as a facesaving potlatch, was given when an individual suffered embarrassment before a member of the opposite moiety. Members of the moiety of the embarrassed person contributed wealth to the potlatch, thus the contributions of the "Eagle tribe" to Charles Edenshaw. This wealth was distributed to members of the opposite moiety and served to erase the memory of the embarrassing event.

7. S'aꞡa, the word for shaman, also refers to individuals who performed in the Haida version of the winter ceremonial dances. The word root, s'aꞡ, denotes "power." Both shamans and dancing society members were believed to be possessed by spirits. By the time Florence was a child, these dances, as she notes, were being performed strictly for entertainment. The s'aꞡá is described by Swanton (1909:160–176).

8. I have been unable to determine the significance of kłiyá as it is not mentioned in any of the usual sources on the Haida. Harrison (1925:87), however, describes a mask (Lthwō-gī-gē or Stlē-whul) which resembles in one feature ("its big red eyes") the mask that Florence calls kłiya.

bottom." I used to really enjoy eating it. At gardening time the men would go fishing for halibut. The women dried the halibut there and used the guts for fertilizer on the gardens. Falltime, in November, they'd go to dig the potatoes up. They only grew potatoes at Yatz because they thought the ground was too precious for anything else. My mother grew turnips in Masset, nothing but turnips, and she used to sell her turnip seeds. After they planted their gardens at Yatz they'd gather seaweed and dry it on the rocks. We'd go back home for awhile after potato planting and then we'd come back to collect seaweed in May.

Near the end of May, ladies would go on boats across Yan to get wild rhubarb [western dock, *k'la q'os*], just like they'd go for seaweed. When I was old enough to pull some, I'd go with my mother. I used to *łkuju* [desire] it so much. I worked fast to collect it and I used to try all my best to get real lots. We'd carry home bundles of wild rhubarb tied up in a tablecloth. My mother cut the rhubarb up and boiled it for dessert. We ate it with lots of sugar and grease.

Ever since I can remember, I used to go with my mother in May for spruce roots [*łing*]. Every fine day we'd go out to North Beach early in the morning before sunrise. We'd pack water and food with us and mother would cook our breakfast in the woods. She used to have kindling ready and she left her pots and dishes there. We'd collect *łing* all day long.

Sometimes, just to do something different from getting *łing* I'd ask my mother if I could get some *xigə* [hemlock cambium] and she'd agree to it. They used to pound and dry it for winter and soak it overnight in hot water before they'd eat it. We ate it for dessert, with sugar and grease. I would just collect a little bit.

When it was noontime, we'd quit collecting *łing* and my mother would make lunch. Sometimes other ladies would come along and we'd have a nice time together—it was just like a picnic. Then we'd gather driftwood from the beach and make a big fire to "cook" the roots. My mother roasted them and I pulled the skin [bark] off. We'd collect piles and piles of them. My mother would know when to quit, when we had enough. The sun would be going down when we started for home. The bundles of roots were all tied together and we each packed a big bundle of roots. When we got part way home I'd make my mother rest so I could pick *sqəltó* [false lady's slipper]. There was just a carpet of it. It was so pretty. I picked all I wanted and when we got home I put the flowers in bowls of water. They smelled so nice in the house. When we got home my dad would cook for us. We didn't want to eat, but we would just to please my dad. Soon as my mother finished eating she'd start splitting the roots in half. She bundled them up and put all the same size ones together in a bent box. She packed them in real tight. She used to have so many boxes to keep the *ting* in. If you don't cover it, the roots turn brown, so she kept them in boxes.

My mother used to weave baskets and hats all winter long. When she was going to start her weaving she soaked the roots overnight, so they'd be easy to work. She'd get up early in the morning and cook and, after everyone was finished eating, she'd go to work splitting the roots again and weaving them into a hat or basket. She worked all day long, day after day, from the time she finished picking and putting up berries till the spring. It was just like having a business. When she finished a hat she put it in a dark place and then my dad would paint a design on it. Sometimes he painted mother's baskets, too. My mother used to weave everything— placemats, hats, baskets with covers, seaweed baskets, baskets for carrying water. She even used to weave around bottles. She learned to decorate her baskets with grass [false embroidery] from a Tlingit lady in Ketchikan. What my mother wove all winter long she sold in June when we went to the mainland to work in the canneries. She sold her work at Cunningham's store in Port Essington. She used to get five dollars for a finely woven, painted hat. Mr. Cunningham paid her cash for her work and she bought our winter coats there. Mr. Newcombe used to come here from Victoria to buy things from my parents, too.

The summer I was eleven, my Uncle Henry Edenshaw had a big doing at Dadens on North Island. The big old totem pole in front of my grandmother's [Amy Edenshaw's] house blew down during the wintertime. The pole had a grizzly bear on it, at the bottom. Jɨtkanj'əs [a girl of the *C'aƚ'lanas* Eagle lineage] made fun of the bear, poking it in the bottom. They said so much about it that my uncle took lots of food to North Island and invited the whole town. They had a big feast with stew and lots of oranges and apples. They gave Jɨtkanj'əs a big bowl of oranges mixed with grease and sugar. Her mother told her to say "*Haadé*" ["people"] real loud as they gave it to her. They wiped her mouth with a kerchief and then she gave ten dollars to ten men of the opposite tribe, one dollar to each. The doing lasted for two days, the ʠənsəngáda. The second day my uncle had a picnic across at Kiusta. He made Emma Matthews and me make sandwiches, ham sandwiches with hot mustard on them. Even though we were little girls, we were real busy. They had soda pop there, too. The bottles used to come in barrels—real big barrels just full of soda pop and funny bottles with round bottoms. The whole town had a picnic with my uncle. My mother and grandmother helped my uncle with the food and they gave him money toward his *ʕənsəngáda*. After it was all over they cut the totem pole up for firewood.

When I was little they had strong Church Army here. There was a Church Army hall down by the beach. I used to go there all the time with other kids. I liked to sing and I liked to watch the ladies in the Church Army. We used to go to church every Sunday. Saturday night we used to bathe and wash our hair, and I'd braid my hair in all kinds of braids. Sunday morning when I'd comb it out my dad used to say, "Jadał q'egəngá, your hair's so big you can't go through the church door." My dad told us if there was any wrong-doing the devil would punish us and that would make me real scared. "Someday the world's going to end and the bad ones are going to get punished," he said. At church, they used to have just men's choir and I thought men in the choir were the very best kind. None of them were bad. When I went to church with my parents I used to pray that when I grew up I'd get married to someone in the choir. So the devil wouldn't punish me.

I used to play with Phoebe Stanley and Josephine Ridley all the time. My cousin, Douglas Edenshaw, used to play with us sometimes, too.

During my time boys used to play together and girls played together, but Douglas played with us because his parents didn't allow him to go away from home. Other boys would go to North Beach or anyplace they wanted to. Once I went to North Beach when I was about ten and my mother spanked me for it. It was my dad's idea for us to stay by home because of what happened to my older brother Gináwən.

We used to play dolls and we played *hʔəntz gudangan*, "pretend." We pretended to talk like grownups. I don't think we pretended at things like *wałał* [potlatching] or *s'aʕgá* [winter dancing]. During my time all the older people were Christians and they don't even joke about things like that. They were scared to joke because it was just like doing it. So they don't pretend. They're scared of God, I guess.

One time we were playing together, hiding, and Douglas came to us with a dead cat. Soon as he brought this cat to us Phoebe suggested, "Let's pretend to have a funeral." Daisy and Dolly Edenshaw, my cousins, and Nora, my sister, were with us then, too. Four of us carried that dead cat and we made ourselves real sad singing "Roll On, Dark Stream." Whenever there was a funeral the Church Army used to sing this hymn. We were all singing and going down toward the cemetery real slow. We heard someone yelling at us so we looked and my uncle's wife was coming at us with a big stick. We dropped the cat and we all ran home.

Once Phoebe, Emma [Matthews], Douglas, and I decided to play wedding in the woods. "You want to marry Douglas?" "No." They ask another one. "No." They were all shy. "Who's going to marry Douglas?" No one said anything. "Florence, you marry him." "OK." We got somebody's veil to take to the woods. Phoebe and Emma put flowers at the front of the veil. They worked at it for quite a while and then they put flowers on their hats that they made out of skunk cabbage leaves, and they made bouquets. All the bridesmaids followed me down to the village. I don't remember if we pretended to have a feast or not. I must have been ten or eleven.

Below the hill called Hijaw there was an old longhouse with three old people staying there. My mother used to cook for them and she had us bring the food to them because they were so old. One time my mother soaked real lots of k'aw [herring spawn] that she had dried at Skidegate and put it in a big preserving kettle. "You girls go bring this to the old man," she said to us. Dolly [Edenshaw] and I and Douglas and Nora went to bring the k'aw there. "Florence, you sit down and rest," Douglas said to me. So we all sat down around that kettle and started eating the k'aw to make it lighter. We did that twice and my mother came out of the house screaming: "Hurry up, before you finish it, and bring it to the old people!" We got real scared and brought it to them right away.

We used to make our own dolls because there's no store here with dolls. The head was made of colored cloth and the eyes, nose, and mouth were embroidered on. We stuffed the head with rags or anything. When I started going to school the missionaries gave the kids Christmas presents, toys and things. They gave all the girls my age pretty wax dolls; we were so proud of the dolls. The missionaries had a Christmas tree and they gave coffee to the adults and cocoa to the kids; they baked all kinds of cakes to eat, and cookies. We sang Christmas carols that the missionary's wife taught us. When someone broke her wax doll she used to bring the broken parts and give the pieces of wax to her best friends to chew. Just like chewing gum. I used to wish for it but nobody gave me any.

When I was a little girl my Uncle Henry Edenshaw used to play Santa Claus for us. "Christmas *Song*," "Father Christmas," we used to call it. We hung up stockings and around midnight he'd come and fill them up with all kinds of things: nuts, raisins, oranges, apples, and bottles of fruit syrup. We hung our stockings in the front room by the door.

At Yatz where my mother used to garden I played with Sophie Marks. We used to make boats out of driftwood bark. We put a stick on the boat for a mast and cloth for a sail. I would sit a rag doll in the boat and sail it in a puddle across to the other side. When the boat landed Phoebe would welcome it. She used to sing while we were playing. She sang all kinds of Haida songs. Sophie used to enjoy the Haida songs very much, but not me. My mother used to sing hymns all the time when she was weaving, I didn't learn Haida songs until I was old. Sophie and I also used to collect chitons at Yatz. She was real active, but I wasn't; I was real clumsy compared to her. My parents used to keep me at home so much, that's why I'm not like her. We pried the chitons off the rocks with a butcher knife and when we came home we cooked them in the fire.

When I was little we played a ball game. We called the ball *sqwəsqáajaw* ["round thing they throw"]. I gathered moss and stuffed it in a little bag made from a clean flour sack. Then my mother would sew up the bag and crochet pretty colored wool around it. We'd throw the ball over the smokehouse roof and as soon as someone on the other side caught it he'd run around the house and try to hit someone with it. The one who was hit was out of the game.

My grandmother used to love us just like any grandmother does. I thought no one could be like my grandmother. She used to like combing my hair when I went to visit her. She used to ask me what I want to eat and she let me eat anything I wished when I visited her.

The summer they first started handtrolling I must have been about twelve years old, and I went with my grandparents to North Island where they camped while my step-grandfather [Phillip White] fished. It was my dad's idea, because my grandmother was sick with rheumatism and couldn't walk anymore. They were living in a tent at North Island and I looked after my grandmother while her husband went fishing. I was real surprised that my parents let me go because they didn't used to let us out of their sight. One day at North Island my grandfather asked me if I wanted to go out fishing the next day. I gladly said yes. I went out three times with him and he didn't catch anything. When Sophie went fishing with her father they caught lots of spring salmon. "You're just unlucky, that's why we don't catch anything," my grandfather said to me. It made me feel real bad. He used to kind of pick on me. At home my mother and dad never said a mean word to us, that's why I couldn't stand it when my grandfather talked like that. Just then my Uncle Henry came to North Island on his gas boat. "I want to go home with you," I told him. So I asked my grandmother and she agreed. "You do that," she said, "you're getting homesick for your parents." I was real happy to get home. I spent three weeks with my grandmother at North Island.

CHAPTER 7

I Become a Woman and Marry (1909–1911)

I was thirteen. My mother didn't tell me what *təgwəná* [menstruation] was. All I knew was "*təgwəná*," I didn't know how *təgwəná* goes. I was real scared. You don't know anything about the blood and you bleed so much. Young girls used to be real shy. They thought that what happened to you was bad and so they don't talk about it; they just kept it to themselves. Lots of girls I knew had theirs way before me. I used to wish I was them. I wished I was lying down like them. Emma had hers before me and I thought she was so lucky (she was two years older). When it happened to me my mother told me not to say a word and to lie down and relax. I didn't mind, I felt bigger. They hung the sheets close to the bed and I lay down for ten days.

During that time I couldn't drink water because it would bring me bad luck for the rest of my life. I couldn't look at the sea because they say if you do, when you're older your face twitches. Eating shellfish also brings bad luck. As much as you try to get food, you can't. During my *təgwəná* they don't let a girl eat anything fresh. You're not supposed to eat much. In the old days they used to give young girls black cod [but not during the *təgwəná*]; they made them eat the whole fish so that afterwards the girls wouldn't be hoggy. They didn't let me talk much because I would get the habit of talking all the time. You have to have respect for yourself, my mother told me.

My younger sisters, Nora and Alice, came to visit me. When they were around they were shy because my parents don't let me talk. I remember someone who was *təgwəná* and she told her sisters to get water, to sneak water to her. The people laughed at her so I tried all my best not to do that. Sophie Marks came to visit me once during that time. Just she and my sisters visited me.

At the end of ten days or two weeks they let me get up and sit around the house. I was kind of shy because I went like that; I was the "talk of the town" because I *təgwəná*. My mother gathered bowls[1] until my *təgwəná*. Afterwards she gave them out to those she loves, I guess. She gave Sophie material and something else because she came to see me.[2] My mother didn't call the women together because of the missionary; she just gave the bowls out in a secret way. My grandmother called the women together when Emily went like that, and for Agnes too. I don't think they did it for Nora; she's three years younger than me; we became like a white people then. They quit it because it's not a nice thing to do to spread the news around.

When I was still a small girl, a girl from Masset had a big potlatch at her *təgwəná*. She was sixteen or seventeen and never got her period, so they pretended and had a doing anyway. She was the only girl in the family and her mother was a rich woman; she owned a store. They invited all the Eagle tribe, even men, and gave out lots of things. Everybody knew it was pretend. Not long after, the girl got quinsy and died with it.

My grandmother used to tell me how I was supposed to act. She'd call me if I did anything wrong and say, "Florence if you keep doing that no one's going to marry you," and I'd get real scared. I don't want to be single. I was small but I thought she meant something real terrible. Here when I got married, I felt so sorry for myself. I used to think marriage law is like tying you down with iron. Now people think nothing of it.

My grandmother used to tell me not to stand up and drink water: "Before you drink water, you sit down." Just men and boys were supposed to stand up to drink water. I guess she wanted me to be a lady. She told me a white people's story about what I should do. A young girl baked bread and had dough under her fingernails.

1. China washbowls were typically distributed at late nineteenth- and early twentieth-century potlatches.

2. Traditionally, a girl was visited during her seclusion by her *sqaʔanləng* (women of father's lineage), who instructed and advised her. Sophie Marks and the other women Florence mentioned who received property following her *təgwəná* were all members of Florence's father's lineage.

Florence Davidson, c. 1919

Her boyfriend asked her when she had baked bread. "Two days ago," she said. And the dough was still on her fingernails so her boyfriend quit her. That's why you're supposed to wash your hands real clean right after you fix bread, she told me. And one time she told me about a young girl and boy who were going to get married. The young boy came to the door and the girl's shoes weren't laced up! Both of her shoes were untied and untidy. "Did you just get up?" he asked her. "No, a long time ago." The next day when he went to see her she was dressed the same. He found out she wasn't sensible so he quit her. "So, soon as you get up, you lace your shoes," my grandmother said to me. She also used to tell me a story about the olden days. In the old days a girl married her dad's nephew [father's sister son]. Before they were married the boy would get wood for her dad, his uncle. And the girl would cook seaweed for her dad's nephew. When the older boy put the spoon to his mouth the seaweed was hanging off and it spilled on his front. The younger nephew was able to keep it on the spoon so it doesn't spill. When she found out the older boy wasn't sensible she told her dad she wasn't going to marry him; so they let her marry the younger one. Sure enough, the older one got married to a different girl and he couldn't get much of anything, but the younger boy used to know how to get things and he and his wife became rich.

Before I got married my mother used to tell me to have respect for my husband. Don't let him wash dishes or his own clothes. She told me not to wash my husband's clothes with mine, to keep his separate. Also she said you're not supposed to wash kids' clothes with grownups' clothes because kids wet the bed. You're not supposed to mix pillow cases or sheets with the clothes, and you have to wash dish cloths and towels separate from the clothing. If you mix them it brings you bad luck. You're not even supposed to wash your face in the dish pan. You have your wash basin separate from what you wash your face in, and when you spill the water out, you don't spill face water where you spill the dish water. If you spill the face water in the pail for the dirty dish water it will cloud your eyes and you can't see clearly. My dad told all of us not to eat too much shellfish or drink too much water. It brings you bad luck, he said; you become poor.

THE MARRIAGE PROPOSAL

When the Indians lived on these islands, and no white settlers were present, their marriage customs were altogether different from ours.

The missionaries came among them, and married all of those living under the tribal custom. The older people have, since that time, arranged all marriages, and this custom is only another form of carrying out the Indian way of years ago. The result has not been to bring happiness to the families. . . . [Deasy, 1915:95]

The girls look for a home, with the surroundings they have been brought up in. The eligible young men are few, and a great number have no homes of their own. There is a custom, among the Indians, of the friends and relatives selecting the bride and groom. In some cases, unhappy marriages are the result. If the girl does not marry, what is there for her to do but to return to the old home, where the elderly people talk the language of the tribe, and where she must again take her place as a helper. She is then taken to the cannery, where nothing good is learned, and many fall away. [Deasy 1917:98]

I was still going to school yet when several people came into my dad's house to propose for my husband-to-be. I was wondering what was going on when all these people came in. The women all belonged to *C'at'lanas*, my husband's tribe [lineage], and the men all belonged to my husband's dad's tribe *Stl'ang'lanas*, except for my husband's brother. They were all streaming in and I didn't know what was going on so I ran to my uncle's house. I told my cousin Josie who all came in to my dad's house and she started laughing. She didn't tell me what was happening. Maybe a week later her sister Dolly got some ammonia in a quart bottle and she opened it and said, "You smell this, Florence, sniff it real hard." I sniffed it and I almost fell down. I didn't know ammonia before that. "You know why I made you smell it?" she asked me. "No," I said. "When you don't want to get married you smell it and you really want to get married afterwards." I didn't know why she said that to me.

"Don't say anything when I tell you something," my mother said to me. "Those who came in last week proposed to you." I didn't know what to say. Propose! Why? I thought. I was just a kid yet. I didn't know what to say and mother advised me not to say anything about the proposal because they were high-class [y'aʌEyt] people.

The next week Josie said to me in English, "Florence, you know they proposed to you?" I don't know anything, I don't know English. "No, I don't know what you're talking about," I said. "They want you to marry Robert Davidson," she said. And she laughed and laughed. I thought she was just teasing me. I told my mother what my cousin said. "Did you say yes?" I asked her. "No, your dad sent them to your uncle. Your dad says he's got nothing to do with it; it has to go through your uncle. You have more respect for your

uncle than for us," she told me. "That's the only brother I have."
"You're going to make me marry," I said. "Yes, you're going to
marry him." "I'm not going to marry him," I said. "Don't say that,
Florence, he's a real prince [y'aʔʕEyt]".

It bothered me so much. For a long time I couldn't sleep when I
went to bed. Every day I bothered mother. "I'm not going to marry
that old man. I'm not. If you make me marry him, summertime I'll
run away. You won't see me again." My mother didn't say anything
though every day I used to bother her. My dad didn't say a word to
me about it. Finally, my mother said, "Don't say anything dear. Your
uncle thinks it's best for you to marry him. He's a prince. He's going
to respect you all your life and if you don't want to marry him you're
going to feel bad all your life. He belongs to clever people; you're
not going to be hard up for anything. We need a young man's help,
too. You must remember that. We belong to chiefs too and you're
not supposed to talk any old way. You have to respect yourself more
than what you worry about." I don't want to say any more because
my mother said I'd be sorry for the rest of my life if I didn't marry
him. I made up my mind not to say anything much as I disliked it.

The night after my husband's relatives came to my dad's house
they went to see my uncle. They asked someone to go there first
and my uncle said they could all come in and talk to him. So they
went in and my uncle agreed with it right away. In the olden days it
was a disgrace for a girl to get a baby without a husband so they
married the girls early. It was a disgrace for the girl's uncle and her
parents, too. They went to my uncle because he's head of the family.
My dad put it into my uncle's hands too because my uncle knew
about the ways of white people. My dad thought I was too young
and was hoping that my uncle would tell them to wait for another
year or two years time. When my uncle agreed with it right away
my dad was kind of disappointed. My uncle thought it was all right
for me to get married because they don't want to lose out on Robert
Davidson. He's sensible and clever and he's y'aʔʕEyt.

It was around Christmas time when they came in to propose. I
was fourteen that September. They proposed for the next year,
summertime, but soon as my uncle agreed to it they wanted to have
the doing right away. It makes me wish I was dead. We got married
February 23, 1911.

I went to school until just a few days before I got married. After
they decide to make me marry, while I'm still going to school, my
mother made long skirts for me. Gee, it was embarrassing. Young
schoolgirls don't used to wear long dresses; they have short dresses.
You know how it could be. I was ashamed to go out.

THE WEDDING

It has been usual for the White race to imagine that the aborigines of this coast are lacking in many ways from the customs of our people and particularly in the manner in which they take to themselves life partners . . . it might prove interesting to describe the ceremonies which [mark Haida weddings].

. . . usually in the afternoon the wedding party starts from the house of the bride for the church, headed by a brass band in full uniform, and accompanied by the men, women and children of the reserve. The groom is dressed in the latest fashion, with a white flower in his buttonhole, and is accompanied by his best man. The bride, attired in white, with a bridal veil and orange blossoms, is accompanied by a party of bridesmaids, all looking charming in their white costumes.

A choir, comprising the membership of the tribe, await the entry of the wedding party, when they sing some appropriate hymn, accompanied on the organ by the choirmaster, who is also a native.

After the ceremony, which is carried out in the English language, the bridal party is escorted to the town hall, where tables are groaning under the delicacies of the season.

On a raised platform the principal wedding guests take their seats with the bride and groom. Tables are ranged along the entire length of the hall, for the whole of the members of the band, comprising 350 people.

At a given signal, grace is sung by the assemblage, and the wedding dinner, which has taken many days to prepare, is indulged in.

It has always been the custom to provide everything new for the invited Whites. The tableware is of the best, and the culinary art of those who prepared the edibles, must be seen to be appreciated. Frosted cakes, jellies, fruits, nuts, and every conceivable delicacy is present. In order to provide the necessary beef for so large a crowd, one of the many cattle, owned by the Indians is slaughtered some days before, and served at the commencement of the repast.

In the centre of the table occupied by the invited guests is the proverbial wedding cake, which is afterward cut and distributed to all present. Again at the close of the supper thanks are given for the good things provided, and oratory is indulged in.

Relatives of the contracting parties open the speech-making by wishing long life and prosperity to the happy couple. All of the white persons present are expected to speak on the occasion, which some do in English and others in Haida or Chinook. After all who desire have expended the necessary number of felicitations, the hall is cleared and dancing is indulged in. . . . An orchestra, consisting of natives, provides the latest music to which the young men and women dance two-steps, waltzes and modern measures. The evening passes in merriment and good feeling. [Deasy 1913:4]

My husband-to-be was married before, to Alfred Adams' niece [sister's daughter]. His wife wasn't healthy; she got TB and died young. I thought Robert Davidson was a real old man. One time before we were married he took me to New Masset to do some shopping. He told me I could buy anything I wanted to. It was snowing, lots of snow on the ground. We went by the beach to town. I walked real fast so I don't go close to him.

After the proposal the men on my husband's side held lots of meetings. After my uncle said "yes," they're the ones who had to do the worrying. My dad sent for my husband's older brother, T'ak [Alfred Davidson], and he told him not to make the wedding too big. "It's not lucky to have too big a doing," my dad said. If the doing was too big I might have a short life; that's what they believed. My dad got ten boxes of pilot bread and lots of apples, maybe ten of that too. Alfred Davidson bought the rest; lots of apples and bundles of "Jap" oranges. The women of my husband's side baked lots of pies and cakes by Alfred Davidson's place. But they forgot to order the wedding cake. Emma Matthews was supposed to get married at the same time but she got a sore throat and they postponed her wedding. So they tried to borrow Emma's wedding cake while she was sick.

The day of the wedding they started cooking beef stew. The young men of my husband's side looked after the big pots of stew cooking outside, but the Raven side helped, too.

Kate Jones made my wedding dress and she wanted to give it to me because she and my husband were closely related, gudʔał qiwa.[3] The day of the wedding the village band came to get me; they divided the band and half went to get the groom and half picked up the bride. Charlotte Marks's father, Thomas Weah, gave me away, not my dad. That's how they used to do it in the olden days.[4] The band played the wedding march as we went down to the church. The groom is supposed to go with his dad's relatives, same as the girl. I don't remember who went with my husband, maybe his stepfather, Richard Naylans, and James Jones. Reverend Hogan

3. This is an important kinship relationship in Haida culture. Individuals who are gudʔał qiwa (ał qiwa, for short) have fathers who belong to the same lineage. The two ał qiwa individuals do not belong to the same lineage, though they would, of course, belong to the same moiety. The relationship is likened to siblingship. Kate Jones later requested payment for the wedding dress.

4. Thomas Weah (also referred to as Thomas Weir in census records) belonged to Sdəłdás, Florence's father's lineage.

married us. I was stubborn; I wouldn't say the promises. I guess I
thought I wouldn't be really married if I didn't answer when they
asked me. I felt bad the whole time. Right after, we went to the
community hall. It was full of people. They made all kinds of
speeches, the *Stl'əng'lanas,* my husband's dad's relatives. They even
sang a song for me composed by my husband's stepfather. I don't
remember the song. Alfred Adams stood up and adopted me at
the wedding dinner because his niece used to be married to my
husband. He said he thought of me just like his own niece. He kept
his promise—he treated me nice all of his life.

The people brought their own dishes to the feast. They ate stew
with lots of pilot crackers. There were apples and oranges in front of
each plate, just like now, and lots of *qawqEł* [food to be taken home
by each guest]. They brought empty fifty-pound flour sacks to
take the things home in. After they cleared the hall, they started
dancing—waltzes, quadrilles, real lively songs.

I didn't enjoy any of it. I felt real bad because I was a married
woman. Everybody but me was real happy. I don't remember any
more about the wedding, it was too awful.

CHAPTER 8

I Become a Mother and Have Lots of Children (1912–1938)

. . . there is no doubt that the Hydah nation is ambitious to become a part of the British nation freed from wardship, and capable of exercising the franchise, on this side of the line as their brethren are on United States territory. Individually, a large percentage of them read and write. They take a keen interest in everything that goes on around them. Their internal affairs are managed by councils, elected annually, and working under by-laws, approved by the department. They have their churches, town halls, good streets, presentable residences, wharves, brass bands, gasoline launches, row-boats, cattle, horses, and all modern improvements including water-works. When at their home towns, the school-houses are filled with pupils, and they are asking for a boarding school, to which they guarantee to send every eligible girl and boy. They all dress well, and the able-bodied Indian asks for no relief, earning a living for himself and his family.

. . . The women are the principal gardeners. They prepare small gardens, before the fishing season, and grow vegetables for winter use. The women and children work in the canneries, for about two months, and the whole family make enough to carry them through the winter.

. . . The Massets did not construct many new houses. They made an improvement as good, in tearing down all the old shacks, along the waterfront, formerly occupied as dwellings, and in removing the signs of former times, the "totem" poles. . . . Since the introduction of the councils, the Indians are doing away with old ideas and customs. The former chiefs are no longer the official heads of the band. In place of the "totem" pole, they have erected flagstaffs, from which they float the British flag. If all Indians disposed of the "totem" poles, and the hereditary chiefs were eliminated, it would go a great way towards suppressing the "potlatch" and the "feast." [Deasy 1917:96–97]

After we married we stayed with my parents for quite a while, till I had two kids. My grandmother Amy helped us buy our first little house. I told my grandmother, "Joshua Collison wants to sell his house. I really want it but we can't buy it." "It's all right, dear, I'll buy it for you," she said. The house was one hundred dollars. She gave me fifty dollars in gold and we paid the rest when my husband went trapping. Summertime we paid my grandmother back. We gave her paper money but she didn't care. We were real happy to move into that small house. It had just one bedroom and the kitchen, but in two years time my husband bought some lumber and added on a sixteen-by-sixteen-foot front room. *Q'atgusge*, we call it. That's where the honored guests are seated.[1]

My husband used to work hard for my parents. He cut logs for them for the winter. Ever since I married I don't think my dad ever worried about having wood. When my husband went hunting he used to get enough for my parents, and we used to fish for them, too. My dad gave my husband money all the time or bought him clothes.

After I was married I used to pack my sister Emily's little girl, Effie, around. "Emily, let me have this baby," I said. I used to dress her up and take her for walks all the time. I pretended to look like a mother.

People here thought I wasn't going to get babies, that I was *q'eq'ala* [barren] because I didn't have my first baby for a long time. When I got married I didn't know anything about men. My mother used to tell me before I got married to keep away from boys. "Soon as you go with boys," she said, "you get pregnant." That's why I used to be so scared of boys. I didn't let my husband touch me for a long time. He told someone I didn't want babies because he's not handsome. Finally, I gave in. All day long the next day I was ashamed; I don't know what to think. Here it wasn't that difficult!

My mother wanted me to have a big family so I'd have lots of kids

---

1. On social/ceremonial occasions the "front room" is the modern equivalent of the interior of the traditional Haida house. The focal point of the house, this room is used for feasts, meetings, and mortuary potlatches ("memorials"). The two critical directional terms applied to the traditional house interior—*k'iaⁿgaga* (the door side) and *t'əcgwa* (the chief's side or place)—are reference points in the front room as well.

to help Henry Edenshaw. Two of my boys used to help him, and Agnes' and Emily's older boys. My grandmother was so happy because all of us had lots of children. In the olden days, they used to give young girls little birds like sea gulls to eat so they'll have lots of kids.[2] My mother used to say, "I want those little birds for you so you'll have a big family." She wanted them for me too because I acted like a boy when I was little. I don't want to eat them so I refused her. I wanted to be a mother for a bunch of kids; as many children as I have I accept it. Today they have two or three kids and they quit. I don't understand it. I wanted a boy first because we had no brother. When I got pregnant for the first time, whoever saw me said, "I wish you have a boy." And I got a boy.

When I was ready to deliver, my mother, my aunt, Martha Edenshaw, and my sister Emily looked after me. In the olden days, my mother told me, women used to take four stones from the corners of the fire and put them under the waistband of their skirts. They get up early and walk toward the beach and every few steps they drop a stone till they're all gone. It makes them get their babies easier.[3] I don't know if my mother did it when she was pregnant with me; I didn't want to do it. My mother was real scared when I was about to deliver; she rushed around, preparing things. I wasn't scared. I didn't know anything about delivering babies. All night long I was in labor and toward morning Alfred was born. He was so big and my mother was real happy. My sister Emily had a baby born the same day, Dora. As long as my mother was living she and Emily helped me deliver my babies. But after my mother died, I got them all by myself.

I didn't have morning sickness when I was pregnant, but I didn't enjoy pregnancy either. You can't do as much work then. When you get the baby, though, it's the happiest time you have.

Two years after Alfred, I got another boy, Arnold. Arnold died when he was eighteen, in 1933. He was at boarding school painting the school building and he fell from the scaffold and landed on a can of paint. He started hemorrhaging. He got TB and he knew he wasn't going to get well. We brought him home and he died in October.

Helen was born after Arnold. She died in 1926 with black measles when she was eleven years old. She was at boarding school at Sardis, and when she took sick her dad went to get her and brought

2. Florence could not remember the English or Haida name for these birds; they are not reported in the literature.

3. Charlie Nowell (Ford 1941 : 157) notes that the Kwakiutl do the same.

Florence and her sisters, 1940s (*left to right*: Emily, Nora, Florence, and Agnes)

her home. She died here in February. Virginia was born next, and then Reggie. Reggie was a small baby; I was only seven months pregnant when he was born. Because he was born way ahead of time we used to keep the fire going all night long for two months. I kept him close by me and pulled the sheets around us. Reggie was killed in 1958 launching a boat. I used to worry about him so much and I used to pray for him all the time because he drank. I was away visiting at the time, in Hydaburg, when I got the news. When I first heard it I thought he'd been drinking and was killed on the highway.

After Reggie, Claude was born, at Watun cannery. Joyce came after Claude—Amy Joyce. After I got up I went to my grandmother with this baby and asked her if I could call the little girl after her. "I think a lot of your baby because you ask me for the name," she said. She was so happy that I asked to use her name. When Joyce was three years old we went up to Ain River camp to dry fish and she took sick. We had been there for one week and got lots of dog salmon. I was cutting and slicing fish all day long. I guess my little girl got double pneumonia; she was foaming at the mouth. She was three years old but she didn't talk yet. That very day she said, "Mum, I want to use the pot." I was real surprised. I thought she was so cute, talking real plain. Here she died that very night.

Primrose was next. When she was almost due I went berry picking with my friend Emily Parnell at Kayang, near Masset. It had been raining real hard and it was just like a lake in the woods. Right above the water there were lots of blueberry bushes. I was up to my chest in water so I could pick those big berries hanging over the water. I kept on picking and filled up a big preserving kettle with blueberries. We walked home with the big pot of berries. Next day I didn't feel like preserving it, I was too tired. In the evening Primrose was born. I had no time to work on the berries and Emily was too busy in the cannery to take them. The kids didn't care to eat them, so all my hard work got thrown out.

My mother died the year Primrose was born. She died in May and in August when Primrose was born I was all alone; I got her by myself. Emma Alexander came to see me right after Primrose was born. She picked the baby up and said, "Oh, I dreamt my sister [Isabella Edenshaw]⁴ came back." That's why she was so happy,

---

4. Emma Alexander and Isabella Edenshaw were *gudʔał qiwa* (see note 3, chap. 7), thus the former's use of the term "sister." The pattern of reincarnation here is much more traditional, occurring within the same lineage.

because Primrose was the second birth of my mother. Just Primrose, Reggie, and Claude were second births. Claude used to say he was the second birth of David Bell. David Bell drowned and Claude, when he was about four or five, used to say to me, "Mum, under the water it's just like on earth. Just trees and flowers on the ground—that's how it looks under the water." Mary Bell used to love him just like her own son. Reggie was supposed to be the second birth of my dad. When he was about one month old he looked at his hands just like he was carving; but when he started using his hands he was left-handed. My dad was right-handed and he said before he died he was tired of carving and wouldn't carve when he came back. People used to believe in second birth [*cants*] so much.

After Primrose I had a miscarriage. Nothing caused it. I didn't work too hard. I was alone then, too. Four months pregnant. Emily, my sister, looked after me. I cried real hard, just like I lost a big baby.

There were five years between Primrose and my next baby, Emily. Emily was born here, in February. I don't know who was by me when I had Emily, nobody I guess. I used to be all alone after my mother died. Gee, that's crazy, being all alone, just like an animal. I was a kind of nurse, I guess, delivering my babies. I could have been a nurse if I'd gone to school.

Myrtle was next, born here in the house, then Aggie. Aggie was born the summer that Arnold was sick with TB. When she was due, I put my bedding in the back room so Arnold wouldn't know what was going on, and I hid myself away in labor. Soon as the pain went away I got up and walked around. I went to where he was to see how he was doing. "What's wrong with you, Mother, you're so quiet." "Nothing," I said, "I was just doing some work in the other room." I got my baby all alone. As soon as she was born I cut the cord and I had everything ready with me. I tied the cord and wrapped her in nice clean diapers, and put blankets around her. Mary Ridley used to come in all the time and see how I was doing. She told me to send the kids to her if I needed help. After I had the baby, I sent Primrose to get Mary Ridley. "Tell her to come in the back door because my son is lying in the front room." When she came in she felt sorry for me because I was all alone. "Why did you do that, dear?" she asked. "I don't want to bother you. I thought I didn't need help so I just wanted to be alone." Everything was all right so they fixed up a bed in the other room for me and put me there. I was staying there for over a week when my husband came home from fishing. He looked after the house and worked just like a woman would work, setting bread, baking, cooking for the kids.

Merle was born after Aggie. We were at fishing camp, Dadens, on North Island. Clara, the youngest was born at Naden. I was working in the cannery there. I was all alone again with both Merle and Clara.

After your baby is born you're supposed to stay in bed for four weeks.[5] My Aunt Martha Edenshaw did that. When I got older I used to stay in bed for only two weeks, but at first I stayed in bed for three weeks time. Right after the baby is born the mother is supposed to drink [eulachon] grease, nothing else. I did that; I love it [grease]. I nursed my babies for a year and a half, till I got pregnant again. Soon as I get pregnant, I quit nursing them. When I had my babies they were no longer painting the eyebrows like they did when I was born. And I didn't pierce my girls' ears when they were tiny. They did their own or each other's when they were small kids, I guess.

From Emily on down my children talked English. I thought it was real smart that they were talking English. My sister Nora told me, "You talk English to them when they're three months old, then they'll talk English, nothing but English."

Emily George, who was maid of honor at my wedding, didn't get her own children. She adopted one of her sister's boys, and her sister Margaret used to advise me: "Dear, you're young and get children so often; whenever someone wants to adopt one, don't let the child go. Hang on to it. It's all right when the child dies because when they bury it you know where it goes, but when it's living, if your child lives with your sister, it makes you feel worse than anything else." That's why I've got a bunch of children; I don't want anyone else to keep them for me. I'm glad she used to say that to me. We always tried all our best for our children. We weren't stingy with things, but we had to look after money or anything else real good. All my life when my kids were small, we managed to get by. We don't bother other people. We used to put up so much food; we worked hard together, my husband and I. I don't think I ever rested to be a lady. Sometimes I used to wash till three o'clock in the morning. Now the government spoils people. If you don't work you get welfare. That's what makes everything different nowadays. Now every month, even if you're not working, you can get lots of money. Life is real easy now, but we used to live good.

5. Four is also a ritual number in Haida.

Florence and daughter Clara, c. 1940

My dad used to advise me not to talk about my children, what they do or how they act. "Don't waste other people's time," he said. "Just a mother thinks her children are cute; other people don't care. You waste their time and they dislike it, especially if your children are ugly." I found that out, because Alfred was ugly when he was little. I used to obey my dad and not say anything about my children when I see other mothers talking about theirs.

My mother used to tell me all the time to have respect for my husband, not to let him wash clothes or cook for himself because he was out working for his living. "When your husband comes home, you have to serve him," she said. "If you think low of your husband and don't do those things, everyone thinks nothing of you. No one cares for you if you don't treat your husband right."

Our great grandmothers believed that even if they don't make enough for a living, they don't tell anybody. If they say anything about it they become like that [poor] for the rest of their lives; it brings bad luck. That's why all our grandmothers were rich. Even though they were rich they keep it a secret. They don't want to tell anybody how much they make. If you're poor and you have rich relatives you don't tell them you're poor; it brings bad luck. Haidas are too proud to tell others they're poor. We just believe in helping other people. My mother and grandmother used to tell us that it pays to be kind. What you give away, it comes back to you. When you give food to others, more will come back to you.

My Uncle Henry Edenshaw used to say to my oldest sister Emily, "I'm old and when anything happens to me, don't be like a girl." Girls are supposed to be helpless; if they want to do anything, the people thought they can't do it. My sister used to say to me all the time: "Don't be hopeless when there's anything to be done. Do like a man would do."

My Husband

My husband's father, Nałang, was chief at Yan [village across the inlet from Masset] and his uncle was chief in Alaska, at Cape Chacon. My husband had ten Indian names, but I only know one of them, Itłagitgwinəng q'Endlas, his uncle's name. My husband gave the name to Father Kreager [minister at Masset, 1965–69]. It means the totem pole, the biggest pole among the Haidas, was so tall and the eagle on top of it was looking down at all the chiefs. That was his real [i.e., inherited] name, but they called him Gəniyá, after his grandfather.

He was real strong and ambitious, my husband. What other men couldn't do, he could. Even when he was old he was the same. He was real clever. He was a fisherman and a carpenter. We got lots of fish but when there was no fish he used to work wintertime for white men, building boats, repairing boats. He built houses in the village, too. Once he made a bed for the children with a headboard and he painted flower and leaf designs on it. My dad used to admire the bed when he came in. "Why doesn't your husband come and carve with me. I could leave him all my tools," my dad said. My husband just laughed. "I can't sit down and do anything," he said. "I'd rather run around fishing; I like going out." If he'd worked with my dad I could have a carved wall now! My husband didn't start carving until he was an old man.

When we first got married, my husband used to run a trapline with his brother Alfred. They trapped land otter and marten, but when World War I started, they worked at a logging camp doing handlogging. My husband and his cousins (George Jones, David Jones, and George Brooks) checked around to get a real good spot to do handlogging. The government scaler would come around to measure all their logs and each one knew how much he was going to get. They made real lots of money. When they finished the trees there we went to get my teeth fixed. They used to make fun of me. "Tree-money teeth. She's real proud of her tree-money teeth," they used to say.

We had about three kids when my husband was handlogging and we used to enjoy camping near where they worked at Awun. I used to save the money my husband made to buy material and make clothes for the kids, dresses and shirts. It was wintertime when we stayed at camp and everything froze up. I washed clothes in the washtub in the shed where we were living and then took them to the creek to rinse. It was quite a ways to the creek. I wrung the water out with my hands and kept myself warm by putting my hands under my arms every little while. When I finished rinsing, I took the clothes back to the shed to hang up. I used to keep the fire real hot so things will get dry quick.

My husband liked working. He used to smoke when we still had only a few kids and then he quit smoking, to save money. He was thinking of me and the children, so he quit smoking. He liked me to dress up all the time and he didn't want me to have my hair any old way. Even two weeks before he died he kept on telling me to get dressed the proper way. So I combed my hair and put makeup on. I put my best dress on. Soon as I came out of the bedroom he was smiling away. "*Wha!*" he said. When you like something best of all you say "*Wha!*"

FRIENDS

> Today at a family gathering I watched Nani and Selina Peratrovich
> sitting beside each other in animated conversation. They speak, they
> listen and respond with youthful energy, but between them they have
> accumulated a total of nearly 175 years, more than two dozen children,
> over 100 grandchildren and great-grandchildren, and more years of
> marriage than probably either would care to tally. Their friendship
> alone spans some 70 years. They are absorbed in each other's words,
> now laughing, now touching the other on the arm. I wonder if their
> Haida conversation reminisces about the early days when they picked
> berries together, the later years when Selina encouraged Nani to take
> up weaving again; do they lament arthritic hands, Nani's "head full
> of batteries," and other liabilities of old age? Somehow I think their
> conversation must be ageless. "We're just like schoolgirls together,"
> Nani once noted. Theirs has been a rich and rewarding friendship.
> [Field notes, July 13, 1980]

Selina Peratrovich, Emily Parnell, Maggie Weir, Emma Matthews,
Martha Williams (my husband's sister), and two of my older sisters
were my friends. We talk to each other about our children, I guess,
nothing else much. I don't talk much to Martha because she's way
older than me. I have more respect for her than that. All my friends
were in the choir and we picked berries together, too.

Women didn't have men for friends. If a man and woman even
talk to each other, the people say that they "go together." Even
today they say that when they know better.

WORKING

The summer after I was married they began work on the cannery at
Naden. The whole town moved there to build the cannery, but we
stayed here. Just my husband, myself, my grandmother next door,
and my uncle and his family stayed. We lived in my mother's house
while she was at Naden with my dad. Much as I wanted to go with
my parents, I couldn't. I was a married woman, no longer a little
girl. The next March someone came around and hired the men to
build the lighthouse at North Island. They hired my husband and
Henry Edenshaw moved us to North Island on his gas boat. We
lived in a tent and I took a little dog, Gwuls, that belonged to my
sister Nora, to keep the rats and mice away. My husband used to
eat in the mess house on North Island while he worked on the
lighthouse but later on I used to cook for him.

In April I wanted to go and see my mother and dad. I was so

Florence and Selina Peratrovich in Florence's kitchen (photograph by Ulli Steltzer)

young and I got lonely. My grandmother said, "If you could row, we could go to Naden." We got a boat and Mariah Smith came with us. She was kind of lazy, this Mariah Smith; she got tired of rowing real quick, and she wrapped herself in a blanket and went to sleep. My grandmother paddled, but I was the only one rowing this fourteen-foot boat. We left North Island early in the morning and it was after midnight when we got to Shag Rock [Yatz]. It looked like my parents had just been there. There was lots of food and dry wood in the house but it was empty. We camped there for the night and early the next morning I rowed us to Naden where my parents had gone. I was sixteen then.

After I was married we went away once to work in the mainland cannery, and after that we didn't go there anymore. When Alfred was about two years old we went to Alaska, Rose Inlet, with my sister's husband, Alec Yeltatzie. There were no fish there. There used to be lots, but when we went, there were no fish and the cannery didn't operate that summer. Usually we'd go at the end of May and come home at the end of September. Everybody else came home earlier from fish camp, but we were still living there with a bunch of children. We were thinking of our children, to earn a little bit more money.

My husband handtrolled at North Island and I enjoyed myself there very much. A Jew came there to sell things like tablecloths, bedspreads, sheets, pins, and towels. The ladies were really excited—it seemed like we were in a city. Everyone bought lots of things.

I used to bake all the time at North Island. We took our kitchen stove with us for the summer and I baked bread and pies to sell to the fishermen. I used to be real busy doing it. Some summers I baked at Yatz instead. Lots of fishermen went there so my husband built us a one-room shack and he moved us there. I had four girls with me, Emily, Myrtle, Aggie, and Clara. Two of the girls slept by me and the other two on another bunk. We used to enjoy ourselves there. The girls picked up small sticks of driftwood for the oven and I used to bake every day: bread, apple pies, lemon pies. It used to be ten cents for a loaf of bread and two bits for the pies. My husband used to bring us supplies for baking.

While we were living in our first house I used to serve coffee and dessert in the front room. I always made pies or cakes, whatever people wanted. It used to be fifteen cents for pie and coffee. Wintertime one year I got a 2½-gallon freezer. I made ice cream and sold it for five cents a cone. I enjoy my life, doing that. Even after I had lots of children, I was still doing that. I don't want just my husband to work for our clothes and everything. I buy the dessert and I get things for my kids, Sunday clothes.

I served coffee and dessert in our second home, too. I quit when the girls were going to high school; it was too much work for me and I was thinking of my girls. But I still baked bread, and cakes when people ordered them. During the last war I used to bake a hundred loaves of bread a day. Sometimes fifty pounds of flour lasted me only three days.

I think just ladies have always sliced fish. The men clean the fish and help with the heavy things. Men think a lot of their wives. They don't want them to get hurt or lift anything heavy. The first time I sliced halibut after I got married, I hung it outside our house to dry and my step-grandfather, Phillip White, came along and teased me: "Qa, qa, qa! Florence, a big *yEł* [raven] has been eating your halibut." He said that to me because it was all raggy looking. Here when it got dried I gave them some. Emily George, my mother's cousin, taught me how to slice fish. We were at Ain River fishing for dog salmon in 1917, the first year we went there. Emily asked me if I had a *tákadaaw*, a slicing knife.[6] "No," I said. "I've got quite a few," she told me, "so I'll give you one." I learned quickly and started slicing away on what my husband brought me.

At Ain, my husband and his brother Alfred used to look after smoking the salmon we sliced. They hung it up for us. We had a real big smokehouse. Alfred and his wife Phoebe had one side and we had the other. Each of us used to dry five hundred fish for the winter. We went up Ain River at the end of September and we came home around the middle of November. We went there during the War years. We were drying fish there in 1918 when everyone took sick with the bad flu. Emily George and lots of others died there. I got the flu real bad then, too.

At the end of April we quit eating dried fish. We soaked it in water and used it for fertilizer, what's left over from winter. We used to go out and make gardens, past Yan but before Yatz. My husband's sister used to go there, that's why we gardened there. Two years after I was married we made a garden there. We also had a garden at Yan and grew turnips, cabbage, and potatoes.

In April when we were at North Island my husband used to go out nighttime for *s'adana* [cassin auklets]. The birds come up on land nighttime and the people make a fire so the *s'adana* comes toward the flame. They kill lots of it, all they want. The whole village used

6. The *tákadaaw* has a semilunar-shaped blade and is considered to be a woman's knife.

to get lots. Sometimes young women go and get lots and give it to
their friends. I didn't have much time to go out for anything except
berries because I was busy with my children and washing. So my
husband did it himself. When he got a hundred he thought that was
plenty enough. He used to pluck the birds and clean them for me,
and I would make stew from them. We looked for eggs too, in the
holes [burrows] on the hillsides. I told my husband, "I don't think I
could put my arms in the hole. I'm scared of a mouse or something
else." "Once you take one out," he said, "you can't help yourself and
you'll get carried away." Sure enough, he was right. We used to boil
the eggs for a long time before we ate them. My husband would
collect the eggs when he was out trolling and there were no fish.
Sometimes he'd fill a pail up with eggs. He was so happy when he
came home with something, all smiles. I used to like it. It made him
feel good when he got anything and I was always happy then, too.

ENTERTAINMENT

> On New Year's Eve Mr and Mrs Henry Edenshaw (Christian Hydahs)
> were the entertainers of the largest party that ever assembled on the
> shores of Masset Inlet.
>   In their large hotel, 26 guests sat down to a sumptuous repast, while
> the town hall was used for the entertainment of 300 of the people of the
> Hydah nation. The Masset Brass Band, under the leadership of Alfred
> Adams provided music during the dinner and for the concert which
> followed. On New Years' Day football teams of the white settlers and
> the Hydahs competed on the reserve. After playing for an hour,
> without either team making a goal, the umpire . . . declared that the
> two "clans" must meet again in the near future to settle in the same
> friendly way the supremacy. From all sections of Masset Inlet the
> settlers gathered in the town and were entertained royally by the
> townspeople and the Hydahs. [*North British Columbia News*, April 1911]

When I was a young kid they used to get me for a bridesmaid all
the time, so I got to dance at all the weddings. My parents didn't
believe, though, in letting young girls go out alone, so when I
danced at weddings my mother would wait for me. That's why after
I got married I enjoyed the dances so much. The winter after we
were first married my husband and I used to go ballroom dancing
all the time. I don't think we ever missed a dance.

We bought a player piano and at big doings the people used
to borrow it. I let them use it in the town hall for weddings and
dances. That's the only time we let it out, for real big doings. We
bought it when we were still in our first house.

They used to invite just men to feasts. During my dad's time they used to invite people with their wives but not too often. When I was young whenever they had a real big feast just the men were invited. My dad started inviting couples to feasts. The first time my husband and I invited the people in we already had children. We invited about ten people. My husband went out hunting and got lots of ducks and geese. We cooked them, and the people we invited were real happy. They enjoyed themselves so we started inviting people in after that.

Once when I was little yet, my sister Emily invited a few people in, including Chief Weah, the town chief. They had a small dining room and I sat the people. I made a mistake and told someone else besides the chief to sit at the head of the table, and Chief Weah went away mad while they were eating.

I used to help everywhere they were making a feast. I'd bake pies and cakes. We used to use lard for cakes in the old days. I wasn't hired,[7] I just helped out. I was real glad to do it. I'm getting a rest from the house, I thought. It was just like a holiday, going out from the house. I stayed out all day long, coming home to feed four or five kids at noon, and then going back. Even before I got married I used to help at feasts, and I'm still baking.

THE NEW HOUSE

Our first little house had three rooms, a kitchen, a front room, and a bedroom. It was kind of hard for us when we had about three kids and so we started thinking about building.

In 1928 we built a new house. My husband designed and built it. It had seven bedrooms upstairs, and downstairs a sitting room, dining room, front room, and kitchen. My husband used to pile the lumber for the house on the beach. He cut the logs for the house and Mr. Robson from New Masset cut the logs at his sawmill. The people used to tease my husband. They saw the big pile of lumber and they said, "Looks like Gəniyá's going to build a cannery." I tried all my best not to buy things, to keep money toward the house. When I buy stockings I keep them just for Sundays. We had a bunch of children and I don't want to run short because we're building. We

7. For certain festivities, such as large feasts and mortuary potlatches, people of the opposite moiety are "hired"; that is, their services are requested and at the "doing" they are reimbursed. It is considered improper to refuse such a request.

had lots of cows at that time. We killed three big cows that winter we were building and we hung the meat on the little porch behind our house.

When the house was finished my husband invited the people in for a feast. His uncle from Skidegate called the house *Naʔa q'Enadas*. "This house is a great house," he said. "The inside is just like summertime; they don't know it's winter out there" [that is, there was so much food, as if it were summer]. That's what the name means. My husband's "grandfather," Robert Ridley, called the house *Ne gut k'iwas*, "the house is right at the road." We kept our home like new all the time. When we had company we served them in the dining room. I used to sew flour sacks for tablecloths. I put two fifty-pound bags together and crocheted lace around the edges. We used up more than fifty pounds of flour a week in those days. We stayed in that house until 1952, when we lost everything in a fire.

The Church

> A reverent congregation fills the Church on the Lord's Day. There is a surpliced choir, and hearty singing. The people have the Bible in their own language and some of the prayer Book. Most of the men, and nearly all the younger people, speak good English; the children are taught English in the School. The men hold Church Army Meetings in their Hall, and Bible Classes are held during the winter. [*North British Columbia News*]

My grandmother used to take me to the White Cross ladies' meetings of the church. Because her legs were weak I went with her to the school where they held the meetings. It used to cost a dime to join and my grandmother paid my fee because I helped her. That was in 1911. I was married in February and I joined the White Cross in November. The White Cross ladies raised money for the church and looked after the church building. Whenever there was a death in the village, the White Cross looked after the casket. They made it look nice and nailed lace around it. Later the White Cross became the Women's Auxiliary and now they call them "Anglican Church Women" or ACW.

When they started the White Cross, all of the members said promises, my mother told me. They had to put their hands up and say "love your neighbor as yourself" in Haida. They also promised not to drink. The ladies used to bring their sewing to the meeting. They sewed things to sell so they could raise money for the church.

We also held basket socials to raise money for a new church.

Sometimes they would pay forty dollars for one basket of dinner. They think nothing of doing that because they want to have a nice church.

I got married in the old church. In 1919 the people started building a new one. There were lots of carpenters in the village and they were all willing to help. I told my mother I wanted to help cook for the carpenters. They made a big kitchen at the old trading company and the women made stew for the men in big pots. My mother looked after my kids while I cooked; I don't think I missed a single day. After dinner I used to go home to wash and my husband would hang the clothes out on the line for me. Sometimes when I was too tired he'd even do the wash on the washboard and I'd hang it out next morning. When the church was finished they had a big doing for the opening.

All my life I've been singing in the church choir. I don't think I missed any choir practices or church services. My husband used to stay home and cook lunch; just once in a great while I stayed home. In the evening we all went to church. Those days young boys and girls used to fill the church so there was just standing room. Nothing else was going on at the same time as church. At Christmas time the choir would start caroling at 10 P.M. and wouldn't finish until four in the morning. Everyone would invite us in. We weren't tired, we'd go to church again at eleven in the morning. It's not like that anymore.

In 1923 they elected me president of the WA [Women's Auxiliary]. After that I was always president, vice-president, secretary, or treasurer. I can't do it anymore, though. I'm too deaf now. When I became president in 1923 they asked me to look after the body of a small kid who died. When Emma Matthews was president of the WA before me she used to say, "I wonder why I'm the only one who looks after the dead bodies?" I knew what she meant when I became president. Maybe I've looked after a hundred dead bodies. Ethel Jones used to help me for a long time. First time I had help was about fifteen years ago when Thomas Marks died. My back was sore and it was hard for me to work on him so Mary Stanley and Emma Alexander, her sister, helped me. They bought everything for the coffin and I lined it and we made the cover. We lined that, too, and I put the lid on the coffin. We put a satin ribbon and cross on the lid, and pleated lace and put it around the lid with thumbtacks. We put the body in the coffin. Whenever I start nailing it up, it's hard for me, thinking of when the person was alive. Even now the minister calls me to go and see the body when there's a death. I go with him to pray for the body.

DEATHS

> For many years now the Haidas have practiced burial beneath the
> ground, a special enclosure some distance from the village being set
> apart for that purpose. When a death takes place, the body is now
> placed in a coffin, and reverently borne to the mission church, where
> the beautiful burial service proceeds as in England. It is customary for
> the village brass band to head funeral processions, playing suitable
> hymns, even sometimes a dead march. When a death occurs, all the
> nearer relatives break forth in distressing wail, which is renewed when
> the corpse leaves the house, and again when it is being lowered into
> the grave. In some cases, wailing is expressive of real grief; in others
> merely conventional. Sometimes to the wail is added blackening of
> the face and tearing of the hair, for these Indians . . . are essentially
> emotional. Occasionally, parents will bury toys and even clothes with a
> dead child, alleging as a reason that they do not wish their grief to be
> aggravated by sight of these things lying around. These extravagances
> are, of course, discouraged by the missionaries, and are gradually
> dying out. [Keen 1914]

There have been lots of sudden deaths in my family, my
grandmother, my uncle, his wife. . . . I was married and Virginia,
my daughter, was about four when my grandmother died. She was
looking after my little girl while I was working at Watun River
cannery. She asked her husband to call Elizabeth Stanley to bathe
her. I don't know why she knew she was going to die. She died
sudden death.

My Uncle Henry Edenshaw died far from home, in Bellingham,
Washington. He was riding in a car and when he got off, he raised
his hands over his head and flopped over dead. It was real hard for
me; that's the only uncle I have and he died far away from home.
Alaskans and Skidegates came for the funeral and afterwards they
had a feast. My uncle's wife said to me, "Florence, you have a nice
husband, have respect for yourself and show appreciation to the
people who came from everywhere and invite them in." I told my
husband and he went out and found our cow on North Beach. He
went there in the evening when the tide was coming in. He killed
the cow and loaded the meat on his boat; it was 4 A.M. when he got
home. Emily invited the people in first, then we invited the whole
town and all the visitors like my aunt wished us to do.

After fishing that year [1935], Emily called me, Agnes, my grown
son Alfred, my sister's son Ernie, and Jeffrey White, her own son.
Jeffrey gave his mother $100, Alfred gave her $100, and Ernie gave
her $100. I gave her $50 and Agnes gave $50, and Emily gave $50
herself. She took all the money to my cousin Douglas and falltime

he went down south to buy the headstone. A few years later when they took the stone down to the cemetery right after New Year's, they invited people from Skidegate and had a big doing.[8] They even had Indian dancing and the Ravens and Eagles had a contest to see who danced the best. The invited guests judged the dancing. That's the first time we had danced for a long time. They gave away lots of things; it was a real big doing. That summer Henry White, my sister's husband, got sick and died. People say it was because we had such a big doing. Too much, it was too big. That's why he died.

My Aunt Martha took sick after she lost a grandson in a house fire and she died while we were down south fall fishing. We came home just before Christmas and there was no Martha. I took it really hard. I was at the WA meeting and when I talked to the ladies, I couldn't help talking about her, too. I started crying. Emma Alexander told me to quit crying for her. "She's Eagle and you're Raven and you're not supposed to take it hard. You've got lots of children. It might happen to one of your own if you grieve too much for the opposite tribe [moiety]." You mourn for your dad or your husband but not someone of the opposite tribe like an auntie.

8. Headstones are not taken down to the cemetery until the day of the potlatch; consequently, many sit before the homes of the deceased's relatives during the time they are saving and preparing for the potlatch. In some instances several years pass before the stone is placed on the grave.

CHAPTER 9

I Quit Having Babies: My Later Years (1939–1979)

I didn't even feel it [menopause]. If you have lots of children, you don't feel it. Every two years I got my babies. You lose so much blood [through menstruation] and you build up new blood every two years when you get pregnant. That's why older ladies are healthy. Today ladies get some kind of medicine from the doctor or else they make them close up the womb so they don't have any more kids. It's not good for their health, I don't believe in that. So many young ladies died of cancer or other kinds of sickness. The ones who get lots of children, they live to be old. Selina Peratrovich and Emma Matthews are older than me and still strong yet; that's because they had lots of children. After I had Primrose, the doctor wanted me to stop, but I wouldn't agree to it. My mother wanted me to get lots of kids, that's why I say no. Way after my mother died, I said no. I could have been dead a long time ago if I had agreed with that doctor.

I told my children not to get married like me. I got married when I was real young. I kept on telling them to marry when they were older. All my girls were over twenty when they married and Alfred was twenty-five. Claude got married young, though; he was only eighteen. He went to Alaska to work and before he went I told him not to get married. I was working at the Masset cannery then, cooking. The local workers all went home to eat but some white men were staying in a house near the cannery and I cooked three meals a day for them. I was hired at sixty-five cents an hour which was real lots of money then because women cannery workers only got two bits an hour. It was during the war [WWII].

One morning, after I finished cooking breakfast for the men, the steamer came. I thought nothing of it but soon after I heard a knock at the door. I opened it and Claude was standing there with a young girl beside him. "Meet my wife, Mom." I didn't know what to do, I thought he was teasing me. I looked at him. He looked so serious. I grabbed Vivian and kissed her. Claude pulled a big box of chocolates from under his coat and gave it to me. "Here, Mom, you have this. Whoever kissed my wife first was going to get this box of chocolates." I felt real bad because I wasn't there when they got married. Vivian's mother didn't know she got married either. Just like they got no parents. I felt real bad thinking about that. Vivian was about sixteen, I guess. They got married in Ketchikan and they moved in upstairs with us.

WE LOSE OUR HOUSE AND REBUILD

In 1952 we lost our home in a fire. I lost everything, even my shoes. No pillows, no blankets, no shoes, no sweaters. All of us lost everything. We had all kinds of clothes and the upstairs was full of groceries we had received from Woodwards in Vancouver.

I was knitting. We just finished eating lunch when I heard a funny sound; it caught my nerves so I looked out the window and saw the shadow of a flame. It was coming from the spare bedroom upstairs. It was Clara's, our youngest's, birthday and we had bought lots of chicken to have a birthday dinner. But the house started burning and by four o'clock in the afternoon it was all burnt down. Joshua Collison came by and chased us all out of the house because the ceiling was going to collapse. After a while, someone came to us all dressed in a white shirt and dark pants, a tall slim boy. I didn't know him, but he asked me, "Mom, do you want anything from the house?" "Yes, in the kitchen there's a blue box, a little box with jewelry in it." The boy didn't come back to me, but later, when my sister Agnes invited us to dinner, I discovered the little box of jewels in my brassiere. A couple of days after, a Seventh Day Adventist minister told me that was an angel. God had sent an angel to me because he wanted me to be happy with at least a little bit. Two of my dad's bracelets were in that little box.

When everything was over we started staying by Primrose and her husband Victor. We had nothing. I was dressed in a housedress and I lost my shoes. I wore Clara's shoes.

The next day after the fire the whole town collected $400 for us.

They gave us clothes, they gave us food, and the Indian agent gave us food. He wrote on a slip of paper that whatever we needed we could get from the store. We saved the $400 for windows. I told my girls we would all work in the cannery to earn money to build a new house. Aggie and Myrtle quit going to school after the house burned; they lost all their clothes in the fire. They started working for the house and gave us $800 toward building.

The fall after our house burned we went fishing with my cousin Douglas Edenshaw on his big seine boat. I cooked for the crew. One day when I was in the galley my husband yelled that they needed me to look after the winch. So I looked after the winch while they were brailling the fish on. I was real proud that I was doing men's work. We didn't make any money fishing that fall, just enough for gas and groceries. We fished around Comox [on the east coast of Vancouver Island] and in the evenings we went into town. I really enjoyed the trip after we had lost everything.

When we finished fishing in November we went to Vancouver to buy supplies for our new house. We bought windows, doors, plywood, insulation, flooring, everything but shingles. We were planning to buy shingles but we ran out of money. We took all our money out of the Fishermen's Credit Union to buy materials and the manager said we could borrow more if we needed it. Because we were old we decided to borrow only $1,000. Even that makes my husband worry so much. We used to pay the loan off whenever we had money and when it was down to about $200 my husband asked if he could pay off the rest with some of his argillite carvings. The manager accepted it and the totem poles are still there in the window of the Credit Union in Prince Rupert.

For a time after we lost our house we stayed in the cannery house where I used to cook for the cannery workers. Right after that they sent my husband away to the hospital; there's something wrong with him, doctors say. They think it's TB, yet he was so fat. They put him in Miller Bay [Indian] Hospital in Prince Rupert for about eight months. When he came home he was real fat and there was nothing wrong with him. He didn't have TB.

I used to pray that we would get a home. I prayed for my whole family because Claude and Alfred and Victor [Primrose's husband] were going to build houses, too. We all started building at the same time.

I used to help my husband on the house. When he was up on top of the house and wanted something, he'd stick a piece of lumber down to me marked where he wanted it cut. I had a sawhorse and saw and I cut it where it was marked. I was young and strong yet. When I gave the cut wood back to him he'd laugh and laugh. "Why are you laughing, did I cut it short?" "No, just like I'd cut it myself, you make it so neat." After the rafters were up the girls did the shingling. Our son Reggie gave us $500 to send for shingles and when the shingles came from Vancouver, the girls started shingling away. They don't let Clara go up though because she's fat and they don't want her to fall down. As much as she wanted to nail shingles with the rest, they don't let her.

My husband and I designed the house. I wanted the front room twenty feet long and twenty feet wide, big enough to invite all the people in. We had lots of girls and when they got married I wanted to use our home for the wedding dinner. Men used to come to my husband and say, "Gəniyá, you're making such a big house. What are you going to do in it?" "Son," he used to say, "I know what I'm doing. Where we're staying now, the whole family comes in and they have to stand around having coffee. No room to sit down. that's why I plan a big house, so they'll be comfortable when they come home and sit around."

I designed the kitchen. At first we had the sink right by the window and when I do the dishes I can see the people going to church. I hated to stand there every Sunday morning doing dishes while people are walking to church. Maybe they think I'm standing there just because I'm curious. Maybe they think I'm staring at them when all I'm doing is my dishwashing. It made me feel bad so I asked my husband to move the sink to another wall, away from the window. "You always make me do something again. Maybe you're thinking I'm your second husband," he said to tease me. "I'm old and you make me work so hard on the house. It's already done and you want everything changed around all the time." When I told Claude and Alfred about it, how my husband teased me, they laughed and they moved the sink right away.

After we moved into the new house my husband said, "My uncle gave my house a name; the name's still warm yet. This house will be called the same."[1]

1. The same two names were given the new house; traditionally house names were the property of individuals. Thus, a house name could be applied to a later structure that occupied the same site or to a new house in a different location if the owner of the house name moved.

MAKING THINGS

> I have to give Nani a lot of credit for my inspirations. I have a theory
> that the women always kind of kept the art alive because they always
> bugged their husbands to do this, do that. . . . Every time I come home
> Nani bugs me about something. "When will you do my bracelet, when
> will you do my ring? I need another blanket design." Everytime I come
> home she bugs me for a new button blanket design. [Robert Davidson,
> August 1978]

After we lost our home in 1952 when we went fall fishing with my
cousin Douglas, I bought material and pearl buttons from Eaton's in
Vancouver so I could make a button blanket. I was the first person
from Masset to make button blankets in recent years. I had no home
so I wanted to do something. I made just one then, working on it for
two years in my spare time. My husband drew a grizzly bear design
for it. I kept it secret because I thought someone might laugh at
me for doing such an old-fashioned thing. They thought nothing
of button blankets during my time. My grandmother used to cut
buttons off her blankets and give them to my sisters and me. As
soon as we got babies she'd give us a big bunch of small buttons for
baby clothes. When I was a little girl and people did Indian dances,
most of them used shawls, wool shawls, when they danced, not
button blankets. Now everyone uses button blankets again.

Haida began making button blankets after the missionaries came,
after they quit raising poles. The missionary stopped them from
doing it and my grandfather was very sad about it. His son, Gəʔwu,
suggested to my grandfather that instead of worrying about totem
poles they should make designs on blankets they got from traders
and put the traders' buttons around the design. My grandfather
agreed with his son, and that's when they made one. I don't know
if that was the first one, but that was when they started making
button blankets around here. Maybe other people, mainland people,
made button blankets before that time.

I've made lots of button blankets. In 1975 when they had the
opening of the National Museum in Ottawa [opening of the
Northwest Coast gallery] they invited me, and my daughter Emily
suggested I give Prime Minister Trudeau a button blanket at the
doing. "You have to do something because they invite you," she
said. "You have to show your respect." I was very glad I got a
daughter to advise me. Robert drew the design for the blanket. I
already had the design and I was making the blanket for Robert, but
when Emily wants me to give a blanket to Trudeau, I used the
blanket I was making for Robert. I worked on it day and night,

Making a button blanket (photograph by Marjorie Mitchell)

about eighty hours in all. I put the blanket around Trudeau when he got off the elevator at the museum. He was real surprised. I gave him a Haida name, Kiłgúlans. He was smiling real hard. "Mrs. Davidson, will you tell me what it means?" "It means your speech is good as gold." "I appreciate that," he said. He was wearing the blanket all evening.

Painting a Canoe

Way before I began making blankets, in 1939, I painted a Haida canoe.[2] A man from the States had ordered the canoe from my husband and his older brother. My brother-in-law was an old man then; he supervised the work and my husband and son Alfred made the canoe. I used to go and watch them work on it, and my brother-in-law said to me, "Florence, you paint our canoe; your dad was clever, you must be clever." I told him I'd paint it. I was just joking but he believed me.

Someone happened to give me a picture of a small canoe with a painted bow so my husband and I started copying it on paper. "We'll make the pattern here at home and we'll go there to put it on the canoe when everybody's sleeping," I said. We measured the bow and made the pattern, on cardboard, in the house. It looked all right. I tacked it on the canoe with thumbtacks and drew a line around each pattern piece. I finished quite a bit and when I started painting it looked real nice. My husband was happy. Every time I finished one part of the pattern, like an eye, he said, "*xwuh!*" He was proud of it.

I don't think women ever used to draw designs in the old days, just men. That's why I was scared when I started painting the canoe. I used to get up early in the morning before anyone else was up. I was ashamed if they saw me doing that and made fun of me, that's why. When it's possible for me, I can do it. All the people were surprised when I was done. Older people came around and said, "Of course, of course, her dad was clever."

When the canoe was finished the ones who ordered it didn't want it, I guess. Someone else came to see it and bought it. My husband and his brother got just five hundred dollars for that big thing. It

2. In 1981 Florence corrected her earlier statement, noting that she believed she painted the canoe in 1936 or 1937. H. B. Phillips, who took these photographs, agreed that 1939 was incorrect and believes the year was 1937, as he was not on the islands in 1936. Because the narrative has been reorganized topically within the life cycle, discussion of the canoe was left in this chapter.

Canoe painted by Florence (photograph by Howard Phillips)

Launching the canoe

was very sad. We didn't have enough money for our food and they had spent so much time making that canoe.

Weaving Baskets and Hats

I don't know how old I was when I started weaving small baskets. When I was young I wove one little basket with a cover for my cousin Josie to keep hairpins in; that was the first one. I learned by watching my mother weave. After I got married I wove a little bit at North Island. Emily Thompson, my husband's cousin, gave me a big bundle of spruce roots. She told me to soak it and she'd help me split it. I made a small basket with a fancy stand and a handle. Emily Thompson gave me grass to decorate it with, too. I made a design with the grass, something like leaves, and sold it to a mainland woman for a dollar. After a while I started making little baskets with covers on them and I sold them to Alfred Adams for his store. In the summertime he moved his store to North Island where the people camped. He paid me $1.25 for each one. I was so happy when I sold him two baskets and brought $2.50 home. I still had some roots, but I didn't make any more baskets because I started knitting sweaters.

My husband was still living when I began to weave cedar bark. I told him I wanted to start a basket and our daughter Myrtle took us along the highway to get some bark. We got lots, but I didn't touch it for two years. When my friend Selina came in I gave her two rolled-up bundles of bark. "Why don't you start weaving," she asked. I knew how to weave but I got no time to do it. Selina started a little hat for me one afternoon. I started working on it and really enjoyed it. Then I made tea while she worked on it. We kept on taking turns and finished it at two o'clock in the morning. We were just like little kids we enjoyed it so much. I made Claude paint the hat and I sold it for thirty-five dollars. I was so happy I felt like I got three hundred dollars for my hat. The next hat I made all by myself. In the old days they used to make hats just out of spruce roots.

YAKOUN RIVER FISH CAMP

When we were young we didn't go to the Yakoun to fish; we got no time. My husband was trolling all the time. He brought me spring salmon from trolling and we canned that. When we got old, that's when we started canning fish up the Yakoun.

We built our cabin and smokehouse at the Yakoun in the forties, I guess. That's when we first started going there. We got ten cases of number 2 cans to start canning with. I sliced and dried real lots of sockeye, maybe more than three hundred. That year we filled a thousand cans, too.

One summer when we were slicing fish, my husband dropped a big butcher knife he was using. I heard it drop, but we couldn't find it. They say it's bad luck to lose something; it means there's going to be a death. The same time my husband lost a sweater. And when we came home from canning, Johnny Hunter, our eighteen-year-old grandson, got killed at logging camp. Not long after that, the summer our grandson Robert's pole was raised in the village, my husband died.

OUR GOLDEN WEDDING ANNIVERSARY (1961)

When it was our golden wedding anniversary we presented the church with a big Bible because of our thanksgiving. My husband was the minister's warden at that time; before him, his uncle, Robert Ridley,[3] had been the warden. All our children were going to give us a surprise doing for our anniversary but it was impossible to keep it to themselves. They all donated money toward it and cooked the food. We invited the Skidegates and people from Port Clements and New Masset as well as the village. We had a hundred and fifty people in the front room and ninety in the other room. We got so many presents they filled up the big kitchen. We unwrapped them for two days.

Springtime the same year the log carrier *Haida Nation* was built and they wanted someone respectful from the village to go to Victoria and christen it. The councilors decided that my husband was the best one to go. My husband said he was too old to go alone but that if they let me go too he would do it. Someone met us in Victoria and took us to the motel. They even used to serve us meals in our room. I wanted to go out shopping the next day and I told my husband, so we go to the hallway to go down in the elevator. "You know how to do it?" he asked me. "Yes, it's written here," I said. I pushed the button and the elevator opened. "*Haw'it*," I said, "Come on." He was scared getting in and the door closed on him. I went down and left him there. I pushed the button to go back up. "It's open," I said to him, "Hurry, get on." Though everything was free for us in the motel we went out to eat in a restaurant. The day we

3. Robert Ridley belonged to Robert Davidson's father's father's lineage; thus, in Haida, he is a "grandfather" to Robert Davidson. At the same time he was Robert Davidson's mother's uncle (a "mother's brother"), and appropriately referred to as "uncle" by Robert.

Robert and Florence Davidson, 1961

christened the ship my husband told me, "Make yourself look real neat, you're going to see all kinds of cameras today." "I don't think so," I said. "We're so old and we're just Indians." I didn't believe him. They got all kinds of cameras and there were about two hundred people at the dock. The log carrier still goes from the islands. The children used to call it *cini* [grandfather] Robert's boat.

The Totem Pole Raising and Robert Davidson's Death (1969)

My grandson Robert got married in Vancouver not long before he came here to carve a totem pole. When he came home to work on the pole I made a big wedding cake for him and his wife and we had a big party. The hall was real full of people and they had a dance. We served lots of things; we gave out fruit and all kinds of cakes and cookies. After that he started carving the pole and his grandfather used to go to where he was working and advise him. When he finished the pole we made a long list of food for the doing—half a side of beef, apples and oranges, grapefruit. The band councilors asked Robert if we could let the feast go and let them do it because we were old. I'm sorry now I let it go; we could have done it, but they asked for it.

I bought lots of towels, all kinds of cups, mugs, aprons, and nylons. We spent about a thousand dollars on little presents. Vivian [Robert's mother] spent about five hundred dollars on hers and Robert about six hundred dollars on towels and things. We weren't going to do it but Phoebe and Charlotte Marks told me, "Florence, don't think too little of this doing. This is the biggest thing your grandson is going to do. You'll feel sorry afterwards when you think of it; all your life you'll feel bad over it. You're wise, but I want to give you advice." I thanked them for it and so we sent for things. The house was full of everything. I could hardly get around there were so many things in the front room. But I needed another big pot. I was the chief cook and I had people help me cut the meat and vegetables for the stew. I wanted to phone a Chinese store in Vancouver where we got pots. Just then Susan, Robert's wife, came in and she phoned for me right away. "Tell him to send it in the air," I said. Next day we got the big pot and all the towels that we ordered. All we had to do was phone for it. At the doing they gave out the towels to the men and the aprons and nylons to the ladies.

Two weeks after the doing my husband took sick. Dora and I had gone to the church to clean. We ate lunch with my husband and I told him not to bother about the dishes. He agreed. When we came back he was real tired. "I'm not feeling well," he said. And I helped him to bed, put pajamas on the wood heater to take the dampness out, and helped him put them on. After I put him to bed I phoned Dixie [the nurse]. After she looked at him she phoned the doctor in Queen Charlotte City and I went with him in the taxi to the hospital there. I stayed with him; I didn't want him to wake up and be all alone. Next morning the doctor came around at ten o'clock with the big machine to check his heart. "Mrs. Davidson, you got nothing to worry about. Your husband's normal today." "Why don't you go shopping," my husband said to me. I only had two dollars with me but I don't want to worry him so I said ok. When they fed him lunch I went to visit his relatives who lived close to the hospital. They asked me to stay by them and fixed me a real comfortable bed. When I went back to the hospital and told my husband what they said he was real happy. Then I went to visit Vicky [a first cousin] for a few minutes. She was in a nearby room. I went back to my husband's room and it's so quiet in there. He was hanging on the railing of the bed and leaning over. I ran to him and I grabbed his forehead. It was cold as ice. "I wonder why you are so cold," I said to him and I looked at him. He didn't breathe. I ran out but I couldn't find anybody. I heard someone in the kitchen so I ran there. "I want a nurse," I said. "My husband just passed away."

At first I just can't cry, it's too hard for me. My husband's relatives came for me and they took me out. I don't know where they took me but soon as I hit the fresh air, I started screaming. I can't stop crying. I didn't go back to the hospital. My, that was hard. He just went to sleep and then he was gone, like nothing. He used to tell me all the time, "I'm old and you should think nothing of it when I'm gone, but you're too precious (*kwoiyas*) to think nothing of me. I know you're going to take it hard," he said. "Don't go out when you feel lonely, just stay at home and try to tough it out." That's our belief, Indian belief. They call it *inda*, denying yourself. You have to keep to yourself, after your husband or wife or sister or brother or parent dies. Not for a little one, though. You have to be alone for a long time, a year or two. My husband died in September and in March the minister told me to go out. He took me uptown to shop for groceries. When I was in the store and looked at friends it made me real nervous. I don't want to talk to them and I turned the other way. I don't get used to seeing other people for a long time. As long as my husband's headstone is by the house,[4] I don't want to go out. When I go out it's like he's there staring at me. It makes me feel bad.

4. The mortuary potlatch or "headstone raising" for Robert Davidson was held in December 1970.

He was eighty-nine when he died. He was a real good Christian; that's why he didn't suffer.

The summer after my husband died, Father Kreager came in and advised me to take in boarders. So I started taking people in; I enjoy anybody's company. I know I've got a blessing, just like my husband left me lots of money. Whoever stays in here gives me money and I can manage for my living.

Right before my husband died, he said to our granddaughter who was pregnant. "Joy, I'm coming back to you. I'm going to be real handsome and real smart, too." Craig, her son, is the second birth of my husband.

Songs

For a long time the Haida quit Indian dancing, but then the fishermen used to try it all the time even though they didn't sing Indian songs. They didn't know the songs. My husband used to know lots of songs and once I pleaded with him to teach me how to sing Indian songs. I was president of the Church Women and I wanted to make money for the church. He thought I was teasing him about wanting to learn. Finally he started singing for me and I learned. I used to ask him to sing for me late at night after we went to bed. Reggie, our late son, used to ask, "Mother, what are you people up to singing so many Indian songs?" When I told him he said, "I thought you both were crazy." Mother and grandmother didn't teach me any Indian songs, just my husband. When my mother used to weave, she sang hymns. I used to know lots of songs but too many sudden deaths in the family makes me forget.

Recent Doings[5]

In 1976 when Oliver Adams was to become chief of the village I decided to donate buns. I baked a thousand dinner rolls for him and put them in the freezer, because his dad was *ał qiwa* with my mother. Their fathers belonged to the same tribe, *Sdałdás*, that's what *ał qiwa* means. My mother thought of his dad [Alfred Adams] just like a brother, that's why Oliver thinks of me like his *sqaʔan*.[6] That's why I

5. Other, more recent doings, which we did not pursue, include Bill Reid's totem pole raising at Skidegate and the dedication of the Charles Edenshaw memorial housefront at Masset, both in 1978.

6. This illustrates the permutations of the *ał qiwa* relationship in successive generations. Florence Davidson is not a member of Oliver

promised lots of buns. Near the time of his doing he came in with my daughter Primrose, his sister-in-law. He asked me if I'd be in charge of his doing, supervise the cooking. "I'll try all my best for you, Oliver," I said. I told him he should ask the people to have a meeting for his doing. They always used to do that, invite the people in to decide what they are going to do. He invited the people in here for a meeting, the whole town. Just the Eagle tribe [moiety], his tribe, was supposed to come, but everybody was so anxious they all came. I went to Rose, my son Alfred's wife, and said to her, "Rose, you're his 'grandmother' [woman of father's father's lineage], and you're the ones who are supposed to be real excited over all this. Why don't you donate money, then everybody will copy you." So Rose stood up and said, "Oliver's older than me, but my mother told me I'm his grandmother." And everyone was laughing really hard. Someone else stood up and gave him twenty dollars and then everybody donated twenty dollars. After awhile we had another meeting in here to plan for the doing. I felt real bad because two of his daughters refused to take part. They're real religious [Jehovah's Witness] and they were against the doing.

When they prepared for Oliver's doing they cut up vegetables for two days and they cut 220 pounds of beef into chunks. We cooked it here in three big pots, outside. The hall was just full of people. I was so happy, just as if it were my own doing. The next day there was another big doing. I cooked the clams, smoked salmon, the potatoes, the smoked seal meat. Claude barbecued the salmon. The Skidegate people donated herring eggs.[7] At the doing I sang a song for the two chiefs, the Skidegate chief and Oliver. The song belonged to Richard Naylans, my husband's stepfather. I have the rights to use it. Next time I have a doing I'm going to spend lots of money on this song so I can keep it. At the doing the Skidegate chief's wife gave me a crocheted bedspread. I got two envelopes from Oliver, one with five dollars for singing the song and the other with a hundred dollars for my two days of trouble with all the food.

Right after Oliver's doing I went to Ulli Steltzer's doing in Vancouver, the opening for her book *Indian Artists at Work*. I was real

---

Adams' father's lineage and thus, by this reckoning, not Oliver's *sqaʔan* (woman of father's lineage). But because Isabella Edenshaw and Alfred Adams were *al̷ qiwa* and thought of each other as siblings, Florence is like a father's sister's daughter to Oliver and, hence, his *sqaʔan*.

7. Herring spawn, a native delicacy, is not found in the Masset area. Traditionally, as well as today, it was acquired from the Skidegate people.

anxious for it. I wanted to see Carol, my niece who lives in Seattle, before the doing so I went down early and stayed by my daughter Clara in Vancouver. I phoned Carol, but no answer. The doing was to open on Sunday and I learned that Carol had been killed on Friday. I didn't feel like going to the doing but I went anyway and pretended to be happy. They had the funeral in Alaska and I flew up to Prince Rupert but I missed the ferry to Ketchikan and I missed the funeral. I went to Ketchikan anyway to stay with my sister. It was a very sad time for me. Soon as I got home I can't get up any more. I was lying around; I wasn't sick but I felt so tired.

> You are cordially invited to a dinner given by Mrs. Florence Davidson in her residence on Thursday, 13 January 1977, at 5 o'clock P.M.

Feast goods for the memorial dinner for Nani's niece, Carol James, continue to pile up. Yesterday Nani removed 2 turkeys totalling 48 lbs. from the freezer to thaw, purchased 50 lbs. of apples, 50 lbs. of potatoes, some turnips, paper plates and paper bags for *qawqEł*.[8] Aggie has baked three sheet cakes, Emily came by with 10 pies and a bagful of candy, Nani made five layer cakes and over 100 tart shells. Tomorrow she says she will set 12 dozen buns and bake more pies. Primrose phoned to say she was baking 2 cakes; Virginia and Dave delivered two five gallon buckets of cookies. Nani has made at least three batches of cranberry sauce and has an enormous pork roast in the oven "because it's better to have too much than too little. I'm afraid the turkeys might not be enough." Merle Andersen, who typed and duplicated the invitations, sent five pink frosted layer cakes, and Sarah (Claude's wife) contributed 17 peach and pumpkin pies. As she was making tarts, Nani noted to me, "I don't know why I'm nervous." I asked if it was because of the doing. "No, it's not my first! I like baking; I've been doing it all my life. It's my favorite thing." Today she remarked to someone on the phone, "My niece gave me a whole case of pilot bread and I haven't used it. That's why I invite the people in tomorrow." [Field notes, January 12, 1977]

We set 80 places at the three long tables, filled cookie trays with cookies, tarts, little cakes and folded *qawqEł* bags and placed them beneath the paper *qawqEł* plates beside each place, and in accordance with Nani's instructions, put 1 apple, 1 orange, 2 buns (on most), and 4 pilot bread crackers on each paper plate. I wondered if the number 4 (a ritual number in Haida) was significant; I know the pilot bread was; it

8. As noted earlier, *qawqEł* refers to food that is taken home from the feast. Typically feast tables are laden with fruits and desserts that are intended for guests to take away. It is expected that no food will be left on the table when guests depart.

had been a gift from the late Carol James, in memory of whom the feast was being given. Nani was consulted on most matters; where certain pieces of furniture should be placed as the large room was emptied to make room for the long tables, where the pies and cakes should go; and what we didn't ask, we received instructions for: "put two buns on each plate, put lots on the cookie tray; they'll take it all. Wait till the raspberries cool more; it looks awful if it soaks into the tart."

. . . After the feast Nani fell asleep at the kitchen table warming her feet by an electric space heater and listening to the tape we made of the doing. As Alfred said in translating her feast speech: "If one doesn't give a dinner after a death one is always weeping. When one gives a dinner, it eases the mind." I think it has. [Field notes, January 13, 1977]

REFLECTIONS

We got telephones first and then electricity.[9] Howard Phillips, from New Masset, asked me after we got the telephone and lights, "How are you keeping, Mrs. Davidson?" "Not too good," I told him. "You white people should leave us alone. You gave us the telephone and you gave us lights. All we worry about is bills coming in. We like to have all the lights on and we like to phone long distance; now we have to pay for all the bills." He was laughing away at me.

We were supposed to get the lights in time for Bishop Munn's visit to the village. They promised to have the village lighted that night. Just before the Bishop came in to our house, they lighted us up. Just imagine, you haven't got lights and all of a sudden you're lighted up. That was the happiest day I ever had.

When I was young people used to think a lot of each other. They had more respect for each other than now. They used to invite people in and they used to bring home lots of food and they called each other "chief." Most of all they respected each other, not like today. When I was little I didn't see anyone drunk; that's the biggest change I see, drinking. After we come to be like a white people, that's what happened. It used to be so peaceful here. The church was full; no TV, no beer, no Canadian Legion. When someone got married, the whole town got excited. If a Yala one [member of the Raven moiety] got married, all the other Yala run around and do work for the one getting married and they give lots of donations to the doing. Today it's different.

Life changes so much. One time you're poor, one time you've got more than enough. All my life when my kids were small, we

9. Electricity was put in the village in 1964; phone service predated it by several years.

managed to get by. We didn't bother other people. Any clothes or shoes we needed we used to get from the sale catalogue in August. We used to put up so much food; we worked hard together all the time. I don't think I ever rested to be a lady, I struggled so much. Sometimes I used to wash until three o'clock in the morning. I'm just like a machine, made of iron I guess. Whenever someone comes in to visit the table was full. We always cooked more than enough and if someone comes in during mealtime, I moved away from the table and put clean dishes at my place so the person can join us. I make myself happy. Even now I still do that.

I always be happy all of my life when my husband was living, except when we lost one of the family. Seems so empty without one. When I was younger I wasn't lonely because I got my husband and lots of children around. Being lonely, that's the saddest time. If you're alone with nothing, no one cares for you, not even your children. That's why, old as I am, I'm still struggling.

One time when Selina was here with me, a nice gentleman came to visit us and he say to me, "Florence, why don't you get married; you'll have a real nice front yard." "Oh, no thank you," I say to him, "I've been married long enough, for all of my life. I don't want to try it again. I want to be a girl now."

I always admired my daughter-in-law Vivian; she looked after Claude, her husband, so much; she didn't worry about anything else but him. I thought she was so nice to do that. I always admire Selina too because she treats her grandchildren and her daughter-in-law [Primrose, Florence's daughter] so nice. I admire Clara Russ from Skidegate; she was so kind to everybody. My grandmother used to say it pays to be kind. "Don't try and save and be stingy with things. You don't get ahead that way," she said. That's why I always try all my best to be kind to everybody. I'm just like other people. I try all my best to be nice to people. Even if I don't know them I welcome them. "You don't have to call me Mrs. Davidson, call me Nani," I tell them. I feel closer when people call me Nani.

Working in the church, that's the most important thing for me. I try all my best for the church, even when I'm old.

You see how it is to be old, real hard. If my hands were all right,[10] I could do so much weaving. If my ears were all right I could be so

---

10. Florence has arthritis in her hands.

happy. *Q'edaəng eʔdu ijing*—"old and good for nothing." I'm just like an old tree. Nothing's good for it. Sunshine makes it crack, and then the rain soaks in the cracks. But as long as you stay healthy you don't feel old. I know I'm old but I still enjoy myself. What I see still makes me happy.

Chapter 10

Discussion

As the personal record of a member of a culture, the life-history document gives substance and meaning to ethnographic and ethnohistorical description. In this concluding chapter, I should like to examine several facets of Florence Davidson's account which offer insight into Haida culture during her time. Her narrative provides commentary on the cultural themes and values governing her life, the options and choices open to the Haida individual, male and female roles, culture change, and the processes by which cultural information is lost.

Themes and Values

In 1975 following a visit to Nani's, my anthropologist husband was immediately struck by the visible expressions of wealth in Masset homes, noting how different this community was from the Alaskan Eskimo villages he had known. Ethnologists who have studied the traditional cultures of the Northwest Coast have often mentioned the native preoccupation with wealth, expressed most obviously and spectacularly in the distribution of goods at potlatches and in the hosting of sumptuous and extravagant feasts. Though the feasts and potlatches have been altered in both form and content, the wealth orientation is very apparent in modern Masset and has been a guiding factor in Florence Davidson's own life. Even a casual visitor to her home can see the importance of property in the rows of mugs and china cups displayed in the open shelves of her kitchen, in the armfuls of silver and gold bracelets she wears on important occasions, in the silverware and plates she can muster from her cupboards to set feast tables for over one hundred people, and in her well-stocked larder, which can accommodate a number of unexpected guests. During the ten years I have known her, Nani has accumulated goods for at least four potlatches and has given more than a dozen feasts.

The concern for wealth, however, goes far beyond the display of property and its ceremonial distribution. It finds expression in attitudes toward ritual purity, work, and economic self-sufficiency, and in attitudes toward children. These aspects of the Haida wealth orientation have been important in the shaping of Florence Davidson's life.

The relationship between ritual and wealth was made apparent to Florence early in life. Eating too much shellfish brings poverty, her father cautioned, and further dietary restrictions that insured prosperity and fertility were imposed upon her when she went through her puberty seclusion. Florence's mother and grandmother instructed her about the ritual separation of male and female clothing and the proper disposal of water used for washing dishes and for the human body. Incorrect behavior in any of these areas was causally linked to economic failure.

If proper ritual behavior insured or at least aided economic prosperity, such prosperity was also to be tempered with moderation. Florence's father did not want too big a "doing" for her wedding, as the overly ostentatious show of wealth was unlucky. Later, she attributed the death of her sister's husband to a funeral potlatch held for Henry Edenshaw that was too grandiose. This is perhaps a strange commentary on the ethos of Northwest Coast economics; there are evidently limits to the size and grandeur of ceremonial disbursement of wealth. The bigger the better, but only to a point.

If prosperity among the Haida was a function of proper ritual behavior, it was also acknowledged to be a function of hard work. The work ethic has been a driving force in Florence Davidson's life. Although John Swanton (1909:50) mentions an ideal of inactivity for a high-class woman in traditional times, I suspect it was more ideal than actual. In recounting her life history, Florence often commented on the hard physical labor that has been part of her life. As a girl she spent long days gathering spruce roots for her mother, helped her father cut firewood, worked summers in the canneries (though she did not view childhood employment in the canneries as "work"), and assisted at her Uncle Henry Edenshaw's home.

Marriage and especially children meant more work and longer hours. Pregnancy, Florence noted, was not enjoyable, because "you can't do as much," but even though she was pregnant for more than ten of her twenty-six childbearing years she managed to "do" a lot. She washed clothes into the early morning hours, sewed for her children, and prepared daily meals for ten or more people. Like many other North American women of her generation, Florence Davidson was also an energetic domestic entrepreneur, augmenting her husband's income to keep pace with her steadily increasing family. For a time she operated a coffee shop from the front room of her house. She knitted sweaters for sale and made baked goods, following Haida fishermen to purvey her bread and cakes at isolated fish camps. Today the loaves continue to flow from her bread oven. "Old as I am," she notes, "I'm still struggling." But when she says, "I don't think I ever rested to be a lady," it is not so much said wistfully as said with pride.

Florence admired the same dedication in her husband. He labored at fishing and carpentry to provide for his family; he made furniture and designed and built two homes for them. And, Florence notes, he gave up smoking when the children were small so there might be a bit of extra money. The family struggled to be economically self-sufficient. Florence remarks, in regard to their efforts, "We didn't bother other people." Economic self-sufficiency of households was the ideal in traditional times also, though I wonder if, in the context of the changing economy brought by the white man, the struggle for self-sufficiency was not greater and the lack of self-sufficiency more threatening to self-identity when the alternative was dependence upon the government and its officials.

Traditionally, much of a Haida family's economic efforts were directed toward its children. Parents worked and saved to be able to potlatch for their children. Florence refers to this when she states that her mother's parents had not potlatched for their daughter, because when they died they were just a young couple still saving toward a big potlatch. Children in Haida society acquired status and rank initially through the efforts of their parents. Those whose parents did not potlatch could not become *y'aʔçEyt*. The same concern for children was expressed long after the supporting potlatch form disappeared. Florence summed up this attitude in her words, "We tried all our best for our children." She sees her married years as time focused upon her children, not just in attending to their immediate needs but in providing for their futures.

"Respect for self," a phrase that recurs in Florence's life history, represents a traditional behavioral ideal in Haida culture. The concept embodies proper speech, proper etiquette, proper behavior, respectability, and self-assurance. It is a theme that not only weaves

through Florence's life, but prefaces her account. Her concern for
proper speech is indicated in her warning that she would not relate
"what's no good." The admonition "respect yourself" was used
on her by adults to elicit proper behavior as she was growing up.
Florence mentions it during her puberty seclusion, and later her
mother told her to say nothing of her impending marriage—
"have more respect for yourself than to speak of it." Florence's
grandmother advised her on respect for self in the proper treatment
of her husband; her father advised her to respect herself and not
bother other people with talk of her children; and her aunt advised
her to show her respect for herself and others by inviting the people
for a feast following the death of her uncle.

Today, Nani's respect for self is evident in her words, her bearing,
her treatment of others. Unfortunately, however, respect for self
does not always extend beyond the boundaries of one's own culture.
This fact is poignantly expressed in Florence's comment to her
husband before they christened a new log-carrying barge in
Victoria. She did not expect many people at the event because
"we're just Indians." James Sewid, a Kwakiutl whose life history is
recorded by James Spradley (1969), provides a contrast. Spradley
notes that "James Sewid commented briefly upon the importance of
self-esteem with reference to his own race and their loss of pride.
He stated many times that he was proud to be an Indian, and the
data which have been reviewed strongly support the conclusion that
he has a deep, pervasive sense of pride, or self-esteem" (1969:280).
With the passage of time, as she has become more familiar with
outsiders through her boarders, Florence Davidson sees herself less
and less as "just an Indian." She once laughingly remarked at the
increasing number of people who have come to know her as Nani,
saying, "pretty soon the whole world's going to be my family."

The embracing of Christianity has been one of the most important and positive themes in Florence's life. When I asked her what
she most wanted to be remembered for, she answered without
hesitation, "for my work in the Church." Anthropologists have
often viewed the church as a disruptive force in native cultures,
for missionaries brought and usually effected great changes. The
early (1870s–1890s) impact of Christianity on the Haida can be
viewed similarly. Missionaries were instrumental in changing burial
practices, eradicating shamanism, forbidding some forms of
potlatching, changing household composition and dwelling type,
and suppressing art forms. By Florence's time, however, many of
these changes had been integrated into Haida culture and she

Greeting Queen Elizabeth at Sandspit, 1971

herself notes that during her childhood all the elder people were Christians.

Christian precepts of good and evil were inculcated in Florence as a child. She remembered only one occasion when she was physically punished by her parents, but she noted that her father admonished her that if she were bad the devil would punish her. So strongly was the good/evil dichotomy implanted that as a young girl Florence wished to marry a member of the choir because "they were the best ones of all." The home Florence grew up in was a Christian home. Her mother sang hymns as she worked, not Haida songs, and her father began his daily carving with prayer. Florence's uncle, Henry Edenshaw, who exerted a great influence on his sister's children, was the missionary's assistant, Sunday School teacher, translator of the Bible into Haida, and, in the words of every missionary who worked with him, a "model Christian." Florence and her sisters were baptized and confirmed into the Anglican Church, were taken to Sunday School each week by their parents, and were married in the church. At age fifteen, Florence joined the Women's Auxiliary of the church and has been an active member ever since. Her present home sits near the church and rectory and she has worked closely with the various ministers who have occupied the Masset post. Her contributions to the church have involved hard physical labor similar to that invested in her family.

Just as she has "tried all her best" for her family she has also tried all her best for the church. She has baked to raise money for the church, provided hot meals for carpenters who constructed the present church building, provisioned and opened her home for church-sponsored events, washed and waxed the church floor, and made altar cushions. She accompanies the minister when he first calls upon a bereaved family, and for more than fifty years she has tended the dead, preparing bodies for burial. Once, describing the church organization, Florence remarked, "We look up to the men as our leaders; we don't question them." While she may not be, nor want to be, a spiritual leader, Nani is regarded by both men and women of her community as an exemplary keeper of the faith and as a pillar of the Masset church.

Christianity has been compatible with certain values and practices that Florence Davidson and many other Haida espouse, and in conflict with others. Reincarnation seems to be one belief that has not met opposition from the church, although the pattern of the reincarnation belief has changed since Swanton (1909:117) wrote that reincarnation was typically within the lineage. Many Haida, Florence included, still believe in some form of reincarnation.

Florence herself is the second birth of her father's mother, and some of her children, grandchildren, and great-grandchildren are second births. Florence's artist grandson, Robert Davidson, asked her recently if she was going to "come back" and she smilingly responded that she would come back through his daughter so "that way you'll have to make lots of bracelets for me."[1]

The traditional Haida practice of denying oneself at the death of a close relative (*inda*) has been followed by Florence and others of her generation, though one does not today hear the old wailing or crying songs and the bereaved no longer blacken their faces or cut their hair as they once did. *Inda*, as practiced by Florence, seems not incompatible with her practice of Anglicanism, though it was the Anglican minister who finally persuaded her to leave her house several months after her husband's death.

Like other Haida of her time, Florence has given feasts and potlatches to mark important ceremonial occasions. In some respects, these ceremonies run counter to even modern church policy, and in other respects they and the church have accommodated one another.

Proper honoring of the dead requires, some time following burial, the giving of a memorial feast such as that described in chapter 9. The Haida long ago ceased honoring the dead with the memorial burning of food,[2] which missionaries regarded as wasteful, and instead hosted a lavish feast of non-native foods. The memorial feast is generally more ample than the ordinary feast, the extra food serving to honor the deceased. The minister, who is present on such occasions, is called upon to speak and/or pray. Feasts have even been used ceremonially within the Masset church. In 1970, for example, Florence hosted a welcome feast for a new Church Army captain and his wife, and when another Anglican minister was transferred from his Masset post in 1974, she hosted a farewell feast in his honor. While early missionaries sometimes discouraged the giving of large feasts, the church's attitude has changed in recent years; the last white minister to Haida Masset, in appreciation for having been given a Haida name, feasted the community himself.

Proper honoring of the dead among the Haida includes not only the giving of a memorial feast but the hosting of a memorial potlatch

---

1. The reincarnation belief does not require that one be born after the death of the reincarnate kin. Furthermore, an individual can be reincarnated into more than one person at a time.

2. Florence could not remember the practice, adding that it had disappeared by her time.

(called in English a "memorial" when I first began study in Masset, but now occasionally described as a "memorial potlatch"). Here the conflict of Christian and Haida values has been most apparent (see Blackman 1973). Though the form and content of the mortuary potlatch have adapted to Anglicanism and the minister participates in the celebration, church involvement has resulted in ambivalence toward the distribution of wealth. Following the potlatch to honor her late husband, Florence remarked to me, "we could have given away more but we were afraid to because of the church." The accommodation she and other Haida long ago made to the church and potlatching was to donate generously to the church, while keeping the distribution of food and goods at the ceremony within limits acceptable to the church. The meaning of these ceremonies, however, seems little altered from traditional times. Florence noted that one weeps for the dead until one gives a memorial feast; the feast eases one's mind and wipes away the tears. Similarly, until proper homage has been paid to the dead with a headstone (formerly a totem pole) and memorial potlatch, the living cannot rest. Florence remarked that as long as her husband's tombstone sat before the house, she felt bad. Only after she had given the potlatch, which followed placement of the stone on the grave, was her mind eased.

CHOICES AND ADAPTATIONS

The options open to Haida women of Florence Davidson's generation were few. Most women married young, remained in their village of birth,[3] and bore and reared large families. The main alternative to such a life course was to marry a white man and leave the islands, but few followed this pattern at the time Florence was married. Florence herself has always lived in Masset, although in later years she has traveled as far east as Ottawa and periodically journeys south to Vancouver, Victoria, and Seattle. Her present home sits within view of the site of her childhood home and those of her grandparents and uncle. From her kitchen window she can see the homes of her now deceased sisters, Emily and Agnes, those

3. Unless they were of very high status and no spouse of appropriate standing could be secured locally. Two of Florence's sisters (Agnes and Nora) married outside Masset, taking up residence with their Alaskan husbands. Agnes and her husband returned to Masset to live, but Nora remained in Alaska.

of some of her Edenshaw cousins and her sister's daughter, and that of childhood playmate Emma Matthews.

The lack of choice in Florence's life is most clearly seen in her arranged marriage. Even her parents felt bound in regard to her marriage since, as Florence noted, what her uncle said was "law." Her initial reaction to the marriage was that she did have a choice. She was defiant, threatening to run away if her parents carried through with the marriage. And while she acquiesced to her mother's request to respect herself and not discuss the matter, at the ceremony she refused to say the wedding vows. "I pretended not to be married, I guess," she reflected. When asked if her reaction was unique, Florence replied, "I don't think other girls were as upset as me." She recalled that her grandmother and mother remarked upon Emma Matthews' quiet acceptance of her arranged marriage to Daniel Stanley in 1911. "Emma must be wise not to say anything, my grandmother and mother were saying." Emma may not have been as vocal in her protests as Florence, but she was not eager to be married. She once noted that her wedding had to be postponed because she had a bad sore throat, and that, taking advantage of the situation, she had eaten a mixture of sugar and snow to make her throat worse and lengthen the postponement.

The Kwakiutl James Sewid, whose marriage was arranged to a young girl close to his own age, expressed in retrospect some of the same sentiments as Nani but without her defiance or bitterness. "I didn't want to get married," he said, "but of course I had no business to try to argue . . . because I knew the older people knew what was right for me" (Spradley 1969:66–67). In the end, Florence had no choice either and became at fourteen a married woman. She exercised some control by refusing for a time to sleep with her new husband, but following a discussion with her mother, she capitulated to the expected role of wife. By the time her own children approached marriageable age, marriages were seldom arranged, and Florence's children chose their own spouses. She urged them, however, "not to marry young like me" and to marry into the opposite moiety.

Despite her rebelliousness at marriage, Florence Davidson identified strongly with the Haida woman's role. As a small girl she found the idea of motherhood appealing. She pretended to be the mother of her older sister Emily's child and wished her own mother to call her by Emily's name so that she might be magically transformed into a mother. Although she refused to undergo a traditional ritual that would assure her fertility, Florence claimed she "always wanted to be a mother for a bunch of kids." Isabella Edenshaw wanted her daughter to have ten or more children; Florence had thirteen, remarking, "as many children as I have, I accept."

At the same time, Florence expresses pride in having been able to perform men's jobs, as well as ambivalence about undertaking such male roles. In explanation she noted that her sister Emily, following the advice of her uncle, urged her not to be "hopeless, like a girl." Charles and Isabella Edenshaw had no sons, so their daughters were expected to take initiative and responsibilities they might not have assumed had there been sons. Early in life Florence was doing the work of a son or nephew as she went with her father to cut firewood. She commented that she was strong, "like a boy." Later she undertook a man's task when she agreed to paint the prow of a canoe her husband and his brother had made; though she had never painted or carved before, she perhaps learned these skills in childhood through observing her artist father at work. Nonetheless, fearing public criticism both because she was inexperienced at painting and because she was performing a traditionally male activity, Florence painted in the early morning hours when no one was about. Finally, Florence expressed pride in being able to fulfill a man's job on her cousin's fishing boat. She admired similar flexibility in her husband, praising the women's work he occasionally undertook on her behalf.

The limitations imposed upon a Haida woman of Florence Davidson's generation are evident in the circumscription of her life. Rosaldo (1974:23–24) suggests that a universal characteristic distinguishing women's and men's lives is the association of the former with the domestic sphere of culture and the latter with the public sphere. While others have criticized this view as too rigid (see Quinn 1977:182), it aptly describes a major difference between the lives of Haida women and Haida men during Florence's time. The distinction may not have obtained in traditional times, but by the turn of the twentieth century men were the primary wage earners and women's lives focused almost exclusively on children and the house. Florence's domestic confinement is apparent throughout her account. Though she followed her husband to North Island and Yatz where he fished, her growing family allowed a little time for picking berries but none for hunting cassin anklets and digging clams with other women. Florence had no time to learn her husband's stories and songs when the children were young. I remember once asking her for the Haida names of birds; she replied that she knew only a

few as she had always been "kind of a house cat."[4] Helping at a
feast, and attending Women's Auxiliary meetings and choir practice
were among the few occasions that offered a degree of freedom from
home and children.

CULTURE CHANGE

James Spradley, in his analysis of James Sewid's life, describes this
Kwakiutl man as an individual who successfully adapted to culture
conflict and change. The push and pull between the two divergent
ways of life is nowhere more apparent on the Northwest Coast
than in early twentieth-century Kwakiutl culture. Progressive and
conservative factions of Kwakiutl society clashed over language,
church, potlatching, and other issues. James Sewid, according to
Spradley, successfully straddled Kwakiutl and Canadian ways of life,
achieving a "bicultural adaptation" (1969:277).
    Conflict is not so apparent in Haida culture of the same period.
From the missionary's and the Indian agent's view, the Haida were
tractable and receptive to Christianity, to white-style housing, and to
the accoutrements of the "civilized" way of life. Yet these changes
did not come freely. Florence's description of her friend Maggie
Yeltatzie, a high-ranking woman who always wore gloves to hide
her tattooed hands, recalls the personal pain that can accompany
culture change. The swiftness of some cultural changes is also noted
in Florence's account. The traditional *təgwəná*, or female puberty
seclusion, that Florence underwent was not held for her younger
sister Nora, because "we became like a white people then." With
missionary suppression of the *təgwəná*, the negative values
associated with female sexuality in Euro-Canadian culture were
impressed upon the Haida. "We became ashamed to talk about it,"
Florence said of menstruation.
    Florence's family—her parents, grandparents, and uncle—had
taken steps to adopt a Euro-Canadian way of life. They lived in
white-style houses and brought their children up as Christians.
Florence's uncle Henry was looked to by the family as a model: he
was enfranchised; his home resembled a white person's home; he
spoke English, was well-read, understood the ways of white people,
and moved easily in their company. He loomed large in Florence's
life both because he was a model of the "new" Haida and because
he was her closest lineage uncle.

4. Older Haida men, however, could recall the names of most birds.

The latter facet of Florence's relationship with her uncle serves as a reminder that the distinctively Haida aspects of her upbringing should not be underestimated. Much of a culture is transmitted in its language, and Florence has been a Haida speaker since she uttered her first words. Neither of her parents spoke English and Florence herself still speaks Haida more frequently and easily than English. The economic values she learned as a child were Haida, not Euro-Canadian, and these are the economic values that govern her life today.

Despite changes in residence patterns (from avunculocal to neolocal) and kinship terminology (from Haida to English), the social obligations and ties marking Florence's life are those of the matrilineal Haida: showing respect and obedience to mother's brother and proper etiquette to other kin; marrying a high-ranking man of the opposite moiety; performing ceremonial obligations as a *sqaʔan*; denying oneself at the death of someone close. When I asked Florence what women she admired, her answer was a very Haida one. The women she mentioned were singled out for their achievements in meeting kinship obligations—looking after a husband, showing kindness and generosity toward in-laws, grandchildren, etc. Proscriptions and rituals which Florence has followed to promote a successful life are also embedded in Haida tradition.

These Haida values and practices underlay the superposition of an increasingly Euro-Canadian way of life, but the two achieved a not inharmonious blend, or so it seems when viewed from the perspective of one woman's life. While anthropologists often speak of the "breakdown" of traditional cultures and the "disorganization" and "anomie" that ensue with acculturation (see, for example, Duff 1964), through Florence Davidson's eyes, Haida culture of her time emerges as an integrated whole, not traditionally Haida, not simply Canadian, but nonetheless a real and legitimate culture in its own right. Early twentieth-century Masset was a good place in which to grow up: community spirit was strong as evidenced in the pride in the village band, the construction and upkeep of the road, church, and community hall. The church was full on Sunday mornings and around the Anglican Church flourished a rich community life into which were incorporated older patterns of moiety reciprocity, feasting, and honoring the dead. Masset citizens were law-abiding and prosperous; they met kinship obligations; there was little drinking or antisocial behavior; parents tried all their best for their children; and the Haida looked to the future.

Florence Davidson's life history also points to some more general characteristics of acculturation. First, her account cautions that culture change may be viewed and experienced differently by males and females. In some instances differential acculturation may bear a direct relationship to traditional knowledge and sex roles. To take a simple example, Haida and other Northwest Coast men entered the commercial fishing industry as owners and operators of fishing boats, a role compatible with their traditional training as fishermen. Women, on the other hand, staffed the canneries and salteries cleaning and slicing fish, skills learned as part of their traditional upbringing. As a result of performing separate roles within the same economic system, males and females experienced an aspect of Euro-Canadian culture somewhat differently. Simultaneously, a changing culture may appear differently to males and females as each retains or acquires new knowledge and experience as a result of sex-role differences that are not traditional. Florence Davidson's unfamiliarity with the Haida names for birds provides an example. In part, one might expect a Haida male to be more knowledgeable about birds than a female, because bird hunting was traditionally a male activity. On the other hand, Florence's lack of knowledge of bird names is probably equally a product of the increasing domesticity of Haida women of her time.

The oral tradition provides another case of differential acculturation. Florence did not learn much Haida oral tradition, partly because when she was a child her parents and grandmother took their newly acquired Christianity seriously, and partly because, as a young woman, she had no time to learn stories on occasions when they might have been passed on to her. Her husband did learn stories, family history, and myths as a child from his uncles, and he passed this knowledge, or some of it, on to his sons Alfred and Claude. Florence, however, laments that she never had time to sit and listen, "because I was always too busy with a bunch of children." Later after the children were grown, she did learn her husband's songs, and from him she acquired other domains of traditional knowledge, such as Haida botanical data (Turner 1974:95). It is notable, however, that in the case of the songs, the main impetus for learning them was in order to stage a performance to raise money for the church.

A second aspect of the acculturation process appears in Florence's learning of cultural roles. We sometimes forget that a significant amount of learning takes place through the process of play. It is noteworthy that in their games of "pretending to be grown up," Florence and her friends, for the most part, did not mimic grown-up behavior that a generation earlier was probably an important part of child's play. They did not, for example, pretend at potlatching or traditional dancing; the rituals they imitated were those of white society.[5]

Furthermore, in a culture that is undergoing rapid change to the point where practices and institutions disappear within the lifespan of an individual member of that culture, much of the memory of the traditional culture is that of a child. Florence's knowledge of traditional marriage for example, is a child's memory. Arranged marriages ceased before such time as she would have been able to participate in the arranging. Thus, she cannot tell of the negotiations, the discussions, the roles the parties to the marriage arrangement played. Her only experience of such marriage was through the eyes of a frightened child whose marriage was being arranged. She has similar childlike reminiscences of performances of the "secret societies." Divorced from the house-building potlatch, which was no longer practiced when she was young, the dances were performed for public entertainment. To a child the masks were real; they frightened and inspired awe, and in that sense conveyed a reality unknown to an adult member of the culture. But the knowledge of the performances, the songs, the meaning of the masks were not imparted to the small girl who witnessed the dances. And that is how a culture, or how portions of a culture, becomes lost to its bearers; the knowledge passed on to the next generation is the knowledge of a child.

Today the childhood memories are critical to the definition and reassertion of native identity. As Pamela Amoss aptly put it in her description of Coast Salish elders, "They now find themselves in a period when people want to affirm their Indian identity and need the old to legitimize their claim to an exclusive cultural tradition" (1981:229). Haida ceremonies barely within Florence Davidson's memory are resurfacing at the instigation of artists like her grandson Robert who create masks, rattles, and drums and bring them to life in dance and song. Florence's description and enactment of dance and song inspire the carver of the mask. The mask is the impetus for the dancer to perform, to excel, and even to innovate. And Florence Davidson, and others of her generation, provide the slender threads that legitimize the masks and the performances in which they are used.

5. During Charlie Nowell's childhood, on the other hand, Kwakiutl children did play at potlatching. Nowell noted that fathers and elder brothers "teach us to give these play potlatches" (Ford 1941:85).

There is no panacea for the debilities of old age as Florence herself laments, but there are some compensations. She has not achieved the carefree state of girlhood, denied her at fourteen and jestingly sought in widowhood, but to her own people and to students of her culture she has become a fragile link to the past, a veritable cultural treasure.

CONCLUSION

Florence Davidson's life history is only a partial accounting of the experiences and feelings of an elderly Haida woman. Certain events and feelings were deleted because she did not wish them to appear in print; others escaped her memory. Nonetheless, the narrative speaks for her; she has listened to it and approved it.

My discussion of the narrative has addressed certain themes and values in Florence's life, as well as the changes her life has incorporated, but it has not probed the depths of her Haida culture, for my knowledge of her language is inadequate. The discussion has also hinted at general patterns of acculturation that may be gleaned from life-history documents.

Florence's narrative offers more than cultural themes and gleanings about cultural change. Its primary value lies in its documentation of the life of a Haida woman. Florence Davidson's life pattern, though, is representative not just of most Haida women of her generation, but the domesticity, the segregation of the sexes, the time spent in childbearing and rearing large families, the provisioning, and the never-ending labor and lack of time for self, speak to a whole generation of North American rural women. Her life history also bespeaks her tenacity and endurance, and that of other women like her. The bearing of thirteen children (some with no assistance), the suffering of many deaths of close relatives (including four children and seven grandchildren), the struggle back from adversity after having lost everything in a fire, the successful accommodation to a rapidly changing world, all testify to Florence Davidson's personal strength. Her narrative recalls the unheralded accomplishments of generations of women who have reared children and seen them to an easier life than their own and who have lived on to an often lonely widowhood.

Florence's own life's journey is perhaps aptly summarized in three statements she made: "I always tried all my best for my children. I tried all my best for the church. What I see still makes me happy."

Afterword

For the last several summers I have returned again briefly to the
Misty Isles on a journey that has become an annual ritual and
renewal. My visit in August 1979 marked the official closure of my
research and writing of Florence Davidson's life history.

I left Victoria for Masset on August 2, 1979. With me I carried two
copies of the nearly completed life-history manuscript (one for
Nani), a genealogy of Florence's ancestors and descendants, and a
"final" list of questions to ask her. It would be a busy short week.
There were old family photographs I wanted to copy for inclusion in
the book, and there was more interviewing with Nani, and the
manuscript to read to her. I wanted to visit Masset friends; I needed
time to touch the sands of North Beach and feel again the magic
that the islands and their people hold for me. I needed time, too,
with Nani, to sit quietly with her at her kitchen table, to laugh
with her, to listen to her. I was accompanied by two dear friends,
Marjorie Mitchell, an anthropologist who had worked with Nani
during the summer of 1974, and Anna Franklin, an anthropology
student who had come with me to Nani's in the summer of 1978.
I was eager to share familiar haunts with them and to see Nani
through their eyes.

Past and present blend as I clamber into the Grumman Goose that
is to take us from Prince Rupert to Masset. Delighted at being able
to secure the co-pilot's seat up front, I greet the pilot, Bruce Brown,
a grandnephew of Nani's, and we exchange news of our lives since
last summer. After takeoff I scan the skies for the first glimpse of the
Charlottes, and watch as the serration on the horizon takes form as

Rose Spit. We fly over the sand bluffs on the east coast, behind Tow Hill toward Yakin Point. The skeleton of an unfinished house sits on the Indian Reserve at Yakin Point, looking not unlike a beached, decaying leviathan. I search below for more changes and discover a golf course beside the Canadian Forces "elephant pen." It seems somehow a desecration of North Beach. The Seegay Inn, New Masset's modern hotel, lies now in a pile of charcoal rubble, the victim of a February fire. We circle New Masset and land smoothly in the cold waters of Masset Inlet.

Our luggage finally piled into a rented car, we drive through New Masset toward the Haida village at the end of the peninsula. I remember once reading an article in a Toronto magazine that depicted Haida Masset as a rural slum. So many outsiders see the broken windows, the faded houses, the weedy yards as signs of a decadent welfare community. I see instead the view from the houses: the spruce-rimmed shore of Masset Inlet, the swiftly moving water, the ever-changing, low-hung skies. Instead of weeds I see fireweed flowers, lupine, and Queen Anne's lace, and by the corners of the houses I see the ghosts of Masset past. I find here a place of indescribable beauty.

"Drive slowly, drive slowly, so I can see what's changed," I instruct Marjorie. New houses catch my eye: Willis White's opulent white house transformed from the weathered frame which stood for years in the Masset dampness, Rose and Alfred Davidson's new two-story house, a brown ranch home beside the ruins of Reuben Samuels old house, and at the point looking out toward the sea the magnificent new cedar-plank longhouse, its carved and painted front already silvered from the sun and wind. We turn down the "church road" now marked by a street sign labelled in Haida, courtesy of a linguist who entertained thoughts of reintroducing the native language. Nani peers out her kitchen window through the foliage of her many plants, and then she is at the front door her pincurled hair wrapped in a kerchief. I hold her tightly. "It's nice to have my girls back with me again," she says. A quick turn around the front room as we set down our bags and then we move into the kitchen where Nani has been frying bread. She knows it's my favorite treat. "*Shibli hʔalingá* [fried bread], Margaret," she smiles at me.

Over tea and steaming fried bread with fresh strawberry jam, I reenter the Masset of now. More of the old ones have gone since last year; the rectory sits empty, the minister having left in January for a church at a Nass River village; there is talk of a celebration this September in honor of the tenth anniversary of the raising of Robert

Davidson's totem pole; plans are being made for a new recreational facility in the village and for multifamily housing. I inquire about Nani's large family and she asks of my parents, my husband and stepson. We reestablish the bonds between us.

Later that first day I explain the contents of the first three chapters of the manuscript to Nani and begin reading to her, starting with her own words in chapter 4. We sit at the kitchen table, joined by Marjorie and Anna. Nani cups her hand over her left ear and leans toward me as I slowly read in my lecture decibel voice. Marj and Anna later tell me that I slip into Nani's voice and cadence. Eyes partly closed, Nani nods, now laughing, now turning to the others breaking through my paced words to relate the story on her own. She balks at my reading of one portion of the manuscript. "It sounds funny," she says of her brief words that describe her first sexual experience with her husband. We try and reassure her that her situation was not unique and that other women would welcome hearing of her experience. "OK, it's all right to leave it in," she concedes. When I finish her narrative, she approves. "It's real interesting, dear." A couple of days later I begin reading some of my own portions of the manuscript. Nani listens intently to the preface and when I finish, her only comment is an authoritative "Right."

I try to fill in gaps in the life history, clarify specific points, and get Nani to reflect on certain topics. We review the genealogy and I ask questions on kinship for a paper I am writing. Nani never misses an opportunity to poke fun. I ask for kinship terms in Haida: "What do you call your son-in-law Victor?" "I always call him Victor." "What do you mean, talk about growing old—you see how I am!" We discuss childhood play again and Nani recounts once more the pretend wedding she participated in. When she finishes, I query, "did you ever pretend to . . ." She fills in my pause, "go to bed?" "No, I never pretend to go to bed with anyone," she laughs.

Nani tells us that when she was young the Masset Haida used to greet each other in English with "Good Morning" regardless of the time of day. "All they knew was 'Good Morning,'" she says. And so, when she goes off to bed or encounters one of us anew during the day, she announces "Good Morning" and we respond in kind. We bring Nani a velour robe as a present and she says she wants to save it for winter but promises to model it for us before we leave. We return from an early morning walk our last day to find her wearing her new robe and four carved gold bracelets. "You look beautiful Nani," Marjorie tells her. "Of course," she retorts, posing among her kitchen greenery for our cameras.

In the early morning of our last day we hike to the Masset

cemetery. The old tombstones are barely visible above the fireweed
and beach grasses, and the new portion mostly vacant in 1970 is
now nearly full. I discover here the graves of others who have died
since last summer. We walk to the beach and sit on a drift log
watching the tide inch silently up in the morning quiet. We hold a
last communion with North Beach before returning to Nani and
breakfast. Just prior to our afternoon departure we gather at the old
oaken table in Nani's kitchen and I read aloud the poem I composed
for her that morning on North Beach. "*Hʔaawa q'uljat, Hʔaawa*,"[1]
she says when I finish. She looks at the words for a moment, then
folds the yellow sheet and tucks it into the pocket of her sweater.

We take pictures of each other standing beside Nani on the front
stoop before we leave. "I don't know which way to look," she says,
impatient at our focusing and metering. "All these pictures are
taking my life away," she teases us. Yes, we would each take back
something of Nani and the magic of her place as we try to record
memories in two dimensions. We drop Nani off at a friend's house
and say our goodbyes there. "*Diman ag<code>a</code>ntł qinga*, Nani" (Look after
yourself). "*Ding sɨn, ding sɨn*" (You too, you too), she replies.

We fly down Masset Inlet, cutting across the peninsula before we
come to Nani's house, the land now to our south. Sundappled
waves lap at the white sands of North Beach and in the distance
glimmer little muskeg lakes. I tick off Chowan Brook, the Sangan
River, Kliki Creek, Yakin Point. I see the flowers and moss that
soften Tow's craggy stone face, and finally, the meadowland at Rose
Spit. I follow the spit to the land's edge; it curls into the sea, then
disappears into the mists for another year.

---

1. *Hʔaawa* means "thank you" in Haida. *Q'uljat* is a term of respect used
for a woman, equivalent to the male *Kilsle* (Chief).

Unedited Life History Narrative

The following passages, presenting a portion of Florence's narrative of her arranged marriage as it was transcribed from the tape, can be compared with the edited version on pages 95–99.

Here, Florence noted that she was fifteen when her marriage was arranged. Her birth certificate and baptismal record show that she was born in 1896, making her fourteen at the time of her marriage. Florence believes a mistake was made and that she was born in 1895. The 1896 date has been used in the edited account.

Tape 5/side 1

MB: So it was *C'at'lanas* and *Stl'əng'lanas*?

FD: Yes. They are all streaming in and I don't know what was going on. I went to my uncle's house.

MB: Henry Edenshaw's house?

FD: Yes. I don't know what's going on so I ran there. I told Josie who all came in and she was just laughing at me. Laughing real hard at me. She didn't tell me. Maybe week after, my cousin Dolly, Henry's daughter, "You smell this, Florence." She got ammonia in one quart bottle and she open it and she make me smell it. "Smell it. You sniff it real hard," she said. I sniff and I almost fell. You know how ammonia smells. I don't see ammonia before. "You know why I make you smell it?" she said. I don't know why she say that to me. I told my mother what Dolly say to me. "Don't say anything when I tell you something," my mother say. "They propose to you who all came in last week." I don't know what to say. Propose, why? I thought. I was just a kid yet. I know I was a kid yet. I don't know what to say and mother advise me not to say anything about they came in to propose because they're high class people.

Next time, Josie . . . week's time, Josie told me, "Florence, you know they propose to you." I don't know anything. I don't know English. She say "propose." "No, I don't know what you're talking about," I said. "They want you to marry Robert Davidson," she said. And she laugh and laugh. I thought she was just teasing me. I told my mother what my cousin say. "They want you to marry that man." "Why did you say yes?" "No, your dad sent them to your uncle. Your dad say he's got nothing to do with you. It has to go through your uncle. So you don't have to say anything. You have more respect for your uncle than us," she said. "That's the only brother I got." "You're going to make me marry," I said. "Yes, you're going to marry him." "I'm not going to marry him." "Why do you say that, Florence; don't say that. *L y'aʔᴄEyt iwan geng.*" "He's a real prince," that's what she said. "*L y'aʔᴄEyt iwan geng.*" "Don't say anything about it." It bother me so much. I couldn't sleep for long time when I go to bed.

Every day I bother mother. "I'm not going to marry that old man. I'm not going to marry him. If you make me marry him, I'm going to run away summertime. You're not going to see me again," I said. My mother didn't say anything. Every day I used to bother her. My dad didn't say a word to me about it. Finally, my mother say, "Don't say anything, dear. Your uncle thought it's best for you to marry him. He's a prince. He's going to respect himself when you marry him and he's going to respect you all your life, and if you don't want to marry him you're going to feel bad all your life. He belongs to clever people. He's real clever. You're not going to [be] hard up for anything. We need help, young man's help, too. You must remember that. We belong to chiefs, too. You're not supposed to say, talk any old way. You have to [have] respect for yourself more than what you worry about," she said. I don't want to say any more because my mother say I'll be sorry rest of my life if I don't marry him. I'm going to just say nothing. I make my mind up not to as much as I dislike it but I don't want to say a word about it anymore. One time he took me to New Masset to do some shopping. He told me anything I want I could buy it.

MB: Who, Robert?

FD: Yes, my husband going-to-be. It was snowing, lots of snow on the ground. We take the beach to town. I walk real fast so I don't go close to him.

MB: How old were you when they came in to propose?

FD: I was fifteen in September and maybe they came in around Christmas time. We got married in February, twenty-third. They propose for next year, but soon as they agree with it they want to have the big doing right away. It makes me . . . I wish I was dead. You know how you could be. He was married before. I thought he was real old man.

MB: How old was he?

FD: He was married . . . he got married around 1907.

MB: And he married Annie Adams, right?

FD: Yes.

MB: Didn't you say you used to take care of their baby?

FD: No, I didn't. I used to just look at him. He wasn't. . . . That's a boy. I guess they got about two. His wife wasn't healthy. She got TB. She died young. I don't know how long they'd been married. We got married same time Emma Matthews.

MB: Same day?

FD: No. She was going to get married before me, but she got sore throat.

MB: Was this when she married Daniel Stanley?

FD: Yes.

MB: Was her marriage also arranged?

FD: Yes. I guess so. I didn't know. They used to do that.

MB: Even after your time?

FD: No. Just me was the last one.

MB: You said that they had to go and talk to your uncle?

FD: Yes. The next night they all went to my uncle's house. They ask someone to go there first and my uncle say that they could come in and talk to him. So, next night they went there and my uncle was saying . . . he agree with it right away. In olden days it's disgrace for get a baby without husband. That's what they used to be scared of and they let the girls marry early. It's disgrace for their uncle or their parents. That's why the whole family . . . that's why they don't want the girls stay single.

MB: In the old days did they ever arrange marriages when the girls were really young?

FD: Yes.

MB: Before their *təgwəná*?

FD: No. When they *təgwəná* they supposed to marry. I'm going to let you . . . if I got little boy and you got girl: "Margaret, I'm raising my boy for your girl." They just kind of joking.

MB: When they're little kids?

FD: Yes. They really got married later. They the ones supposed to marry each others. If they haven't got any for the chief's family. If I was chief and you my wife and we got grownup girl and someone else from different village, chiefs, they come to ask you if they can get married to your daughter. They agree with each other and they get married right there at the girl's home town. The girl not supposed to go to the man's. They always come for the girl.

MB: When your grandmother was married to Albert Edward Edenshaw, did they have a doing in Klinkwan or not?

FD: No, they took them home to get married to her. He didn't marry her at Klinkwan. He took the girls to his home town for his doing in Naden. They didn't go to bed together unless they get married. They have big ceremony like nowadays. They would propose to the girl and the day they set the day and they have the girl. I'm supposed to be princess now, head of the house. They put the mattress there and the girl with new clothes on sitting there at the head of the house.

MB: In the old days?

FD: Yes. All the people who came in for the feast they sitting around on the *day cindu*. They all sitting around there and they take the boy in.

MB: The girl's in the back of the house in the chief's place in the rear part of the house?

FD: Yes. The longhouse this way and here's the back of the house and there's partition there, just like bedroom. Front of that the chief and his wife used to sit there. When their daughter gets married and when they come in from the other chief's house with the boy just like how they come in to propose. The boy come in, the young boy would come in with his uncle or with his dad. They all relative go in after them. They have the room for them where they're going to sit. They bring the boy in. They make him sit down by the girl.

MB: Is the girl sitting by her parents?

FD: Yes. I guess her parents are there with her. They bring the boy in and they make them sit together and they serve meal then.

BIBLIOGRAPHY

Amoss, Pamela
   1981   "Coast Salish Elders." In *Other Ways of Growing Old: Anthropo-logical Perspectives*, edited by Pamela Amoss and Stevan Harrell, pp. 227–477. Stanford: Stanford University Press.
Appleton, F. M.
   1970   "Life and Art of Charlie Edenshaw." *Canadian Geographical Journal* 81:20–25.
Barbeau, Marius
   1944   "How Raven Stole the Sun: Charles Edenshaw's Argillite Carvings." *Transactions of the Royal Society of Canada* (ser. 3) 38:59–69.
   1957   *Haida Carvers in Argillite*. National Museum of Man, Bulletin 139. Ottawa.
Bartlett, John
   1925   "A Narrative of Events in the Life of John Bartlett." In *The Sea, the Ship, the Sailor*. Salem, Mass.: Marine Research Society.
Blackman, Margaret
   1973   "Totems to Tombstones: Culture Change as Viewed through the Haida Mortuary Complex, 1877–1971." *Ethnology* 12:47–56.
   1977   "Ethnohistoric Changes in the Haida Potlatch Complex." *Arctic Anthropology* 14:39–53.
Boas, Franz
   1943   "Recent Anthropology." *Science* 98:311–14, 334–37.
The British Colonist
   1862   "The Smallpox," May 13, p.3.
            "From Bentinek Arm, Fort Rupert and Nanaimo," June 21, p.3.
Brumble, H. David
   1981   *An Annotated Bibliography of American Indian and Eskimo Auto-biographies*. Lincoln: University of Nebraska Press.

Campbell, Maria
  1973   *Halfbreed.* Toronto: McClelland and Stewart, Ltd.
Collison, William H.
  1915   *In the Wake of the War Canoe.* London: Seeley, Service and Co., Ltd.
Curtis, Edward S.
  1916   *The Haida. The North American Indian,* vol. 11, pp. 115–75, 186–93. Norwood, Illinois.
Dawson, George
  1880   *Report on the Queen Charlotte Islands.* Geological Survey of Canada, Report of Progress for 1878–79.
Deans, James
  1891   "Carved Columns or Totem Poles of the Haidas." *American Antiquarian and Oriental Journal* 13:282–87.
Deasy, Thomas
  1913   "How the Haida Indians Celebrate Weddings." *Masset Leader* (February 6, 1913), 1(21):4.
  1915   Report of Thomas Deasy, Indian Agent for Queen Charlotte Agency, British Columbia. *Annual Report of the Department of Indian Affairs,* Canada.
  1917   Report of Thomas Deasy, Indian Agent for Queen Charlotte Agency, British Columbia. *Annual Report of the Department of Indian Affairs,* Canada.
Dixon, George
  1789   *A Voyage Round the World . . .* London.
Dougherty, Molly
  1978   *Becoming a Woman in Rural Black Culture.* New York: Holt, Rinehart and Winston.
Du Vernet, ?
  1906   Letter, December 20, 1906. Church Missionary Society Archives, London.
Duff, Wilson
  n.d.   Unpublished field notes on the Haida.
  1964   *The Indian History of British Columbia.* Vol. 1: *The Impact of the White Man.* Anthropology in British Columbia, Memoir 5. Victoria, B.C.: Provincial Museum.
Dunn, J.
  1846   *History of the Oregon Territory.* London.
Ford, Clellan
  1941   *Smoke From Their Fires: The Life of a Kwakiutl Chief.* New Haven: Yale University Press.
Green, Jonathan
  1915   *Journal of a Tour on the Northwest Coast of America in the year 1829.* New York: Charles Heartman.
Harrison, Charles
  1911–   History of the Queen Charlotte Islands: The Haida and Their
  13   Legends. *Queen Charlotte Islander,* vol. I, no. 11 (November 6, 1911)—vol. II, no. 34 (April 28, 1913).

1925 *Ancient Warriors of the North Pacific*. London.

Holm, Bill

1981 "Will the Real Charles Edensaw Please Stand Up?: The Problem of Attribution in Northwest Coast Indian Art." In *The World Is as Sharp as a Knife: An Anthology in Honour of Wilson Duff*, edited by Donald N. Abbott, pp. 175–200. Victoria, B.C.: Provincial Museum.

Howay, F. W., ed.

1941 *Voyages of the* Columbia *to the Northwest Coast, 1787–1790 and 1790–1793*. Boston: Massachusetts Historical Society.

Ingraham, J.

1971 *Joseph Ingraham's Journal of the Brigantine* Hope *on a Voyage to the Northwest Coast of North America, 1790–92*. Edited, with notes and an Introduction by Mark D. Kaplanoff. Barre, Mass.: Imprint Society.

Jackson, Sheldon

1880 *Alaska and Missions on the North Pacific Coast*. New York: Dodd, Mead and Company.

Jamieson, Kathleen

1978 *Indian Women and the Law in Canada: Citizens Minus*. Canada: Advisory Council on the Status of Women, Indian Rights for Indian Women.

Jelinek, Estelle

1980 "Women's Autobiography and the Male Tradition." In *Women's Autobiography: Essays in Criticism*, edited by Estelle Jelinek, pp. 1–20. Bloomington: Indiana University Press.

Jenness, Diamond

1955 *The Faith of a Coast Salish Indian*. Anthropology in British Columbia, Memoir 3, pp. 1–92. Victoria, B.C.: Provincial Museum.

Jones, Rex, and Shirley Jones

1976 *The Himalayan Woman*. Palo Alto: Mayfield Publishing Company.

Keen, J. H.

1894 Letter, May 28, 1894. Church Missionary Society Archives, London.

1914 "Haida Burial." *North British Columbia News*, vol. 4, no. 17:6.

Kelley, Jane

1978 *Yaqui Women: Contemporary Life Histories*. Lincoln: University of Nebraska Press.

Kluckhohn, Clyde

1945 "The Personal Document in Anthropological Science." In *The Use of Personal Documents in History, Anthropology, and Sociology*, edited by Louis Gottschalk et al., pp. 79–175. Social Science Research Council, Bulletin 53.

Krause, A.

1885 *The Tlingit Indians*. Translated by Erna Gunther. Seattle: University of Washington Press.

Kroeber, A. L.
  1908   "War Experiences of Individuals." In *Ethnology of the Gros Ventre.*
          Anthropological Papers of the American Museum of Natural
          History 1(4):196–222.
La Pérouse, J. F. G. de
  1798   *The Voyage of La Pérouse Round the World in the Years 1785, 1786,
          1787, and 1788, with the Nautical Tables.* Arranged by M. L. A.
          Milet Mureau at Paris. Translated from the French in two vols.
          London: John Stockdale.
Langness, L. I.
  1965   *The Life History in Anthropological Science.* New York: Holt,
          Rinehart and Winston.
Langness, L. I., and Gelya Frank
  1981   *Lives: An Anthropological Approach to Biography.* Novato, Calif.:
          Chandler and Sharp.
Lawrence, Erma
  1977   *Haida Dictionary.* Fairbanks: Alaska Native Language Center.
Levine, Robert
  1973   "Notes on a Haida Text." *The Charlottes: A Journal of the Queen
          Charlotte Islands,* vol. 2, pp. 28–32.
Liberty, Margot
  1978   *American Indian Intellectuals.* 1976 Proceedings of the American
          Ethnological Society.
Lurie, Nancy
  1961   *Mountain Wolf Woman, Sister of Crashing Thunder. Autobiography of a
          Winnebago Indian.* Ann Arbor: University of Michigan Press.
Marchand, Etienne
  1801   *A Voyage Round the World Performed during the Years 1790, 1791, and
          1792.* 2 vols. London: T. N. Longman.
Martin, M. K., and B. Voorhies
  1975   *Female of the Species.* New York: Columbia University Press.
Mead, Margaret
  1972   *Blackberry Winter.* New York: William Morrow.
Mitchell, Marjorie
  1976   "Women, Poverty, and Housing: Some Consequences of
          Hinterland Status for a Coast Salish Indian Reserve in
          Metropolitan Canada." Ph.D. dissertation, Department of
          Anthropology, University of British Columbia.
Morley, Alan Palmer
  1967   *Roar of the Breakers: A Biography of Peter Kelly.* Toronto: Ryerson
          Press.
Murdock, George Peter
  1934a   "Kinship and Social Behavior Among the Haida." *American
          Anthropologist* 36:355–85.
  1934b   "The Haidas of British Columbia." In *Our Primitive Contemporaries,*
          edited by George Peter Murdock, New York: McGraw Hill.

1936   *Rank and Potlatch Among the Haida.* Yale University Publications in Anthropology, no. 13.

Neithammer, Carolyn

1977   *Daughters of the Earth: The Lives and Legends of American Indian Women.* New York: Collier.

North British Columbia News

1911   "Holiday Doings at Masset." Vol. 6, p. 71 (April, 1911).

Panday, Trikoli Nath

1978   "Flora Zuni, Zuni, 1897–." In *American Indian Intellectuals,* edited by Margot Liberty, pp. 217–25. 1976 Proceedings of the American Ethnological Society.

Parsons, Elsie Clews, ed.

1922   *American Indian Life.* New York: B. W. Huebsch, Inc.

Phillips, Herbert

1973   Comment on David Mandelbaum's *The Study of Life History: Gandhi. Current Anthropology* 14:200–201.

Poewe, Karla

1981   *Matrilineal Ideology: Male-Female Dynamics in Luapula, Zambia.* New York: Academic Press.

Pomerleau, Cynthia

1980   "The Emergence of Women's Autobiography in England." In *Women's Autobiography: Essays in Criticism,* edited by Estelle Jelinek, pp. 1–20. Bloomington: Indiana University Press.

Poole, Francis

1872   *Queen Charlotte Islands: A Narrative of Discovery and Adventure in the North Pacific.* London: Hurst and Blacklett.

Quinn, Nancy

1977   "Anthropological Studies on Women's Status." *Annual Review of Anthropology* 6:181–225.

Radin, Paul

1913   "Personal Reminiscences of a Winnebago Indian." *Journal of American Folklore* 26:293–318.

Robinson, Michael P.

1978   *Sea Otter Chiefs.* Vancouver: Friendly Cove Press.

Rohner, Ronald

1966   "Franz Boas: Ethnographer on the Northwest Coast." In *Pioneers of American Anthropology: The Uses of Biography,* edited by June Helm, pp. 149–212. Seattle and London: University of Washington Press.

Rosaldo, Michelle

1974   "Women, Culture, and Society: A Theoretical Overview." In *Women, Culture and Society,* edited by M. Rosaldo and L. Lamphere, pp. 17–42. Stanford: Stanford University Press.

Rosman, Abraham, and Paula Rubel

1971   *Feasting with Mine Enemy: Rank and Exchange Among Northwest Coast Societies.* New York: Columbia University Press.

Spradley, James
    1969   *Guests Never Leave Hungry: The Autobiography of James Sewid, a Kwakiutl Indian.* New Haven: Yale University Press.
Stearns, Mary Lee
    1975   "Life Cycle Rituals of the Modern Haida." In *Contributions to Canadian Ethnology*, no. 31, edited by David Carlisle, pp. 129–69. Ottawa: National Museums of Canada.
    1981   *Haida Culture in Custody: The Masset Band.* Seattle and London: University of Washington Press.
Steltzer, Ulli
    1976   *Indian Artists at Work.* Seattle: University of Washington Press; Vancouver, B.C.: Douglas and McIntyre.
Strathern, Marilyn
    1972   *Women in Between: Female Roles in a Male World.* New York: Seminar Press.
Swan, James
    1883   Journal of a Trip to Queen Charlotte Islands, B.C. Microfilm. Seattle: University of Washington Library.
Swanton, John R.
    1909   *Contributions to the Ethnology of the Haida.* American Museum of Natural History, Memoir 8.
Turner, Nancy
    1974   "Plant Taxonomic Systems and Ethnobotany of Three Contemporary Indian Groups of the Pacific Northwest (Haida, Bella Coola, and Lillooet)." *Syesis*, vol. 7, supplement 1.
Underhill, Ruth
    1936   *The Autobiography of a Papago Woman.* Memoirs of the American Anthropological Association, no. 46.
Vanderburgh, R. M.
    1977   *I Am Nokomis Too: The Biography of Vera Patronella Johnson.* Don Mills, Ontario: General Publishing Company, Ltd.
Wagner, Henry R., and W. A. Newcombe, eds.
    1938   "The Journal of Jacinto Caamaño." Translated by Capt. Harold Grenfell, R.N. *British Columbia Historical Quarterly* 2:189–222, 265–301.
Weiner, Annette
    1976   *Women of Value, Men of Renown: New Perspectives in Trobriand Exchange.* Austin: University of Texas Press.
Wike, Joyce
    1951   "The Effect of the Maritime Fur Trade on the Northwest Coast Indian Societies." Ph.D. dissertation, Department of Anthropology, Columbia University.
Willis, Jane
    1973   *Geniesh: An Indian Girlhood.* Toronto: New Press.

Index

The page numbers for illustrations are given in boldface type.

Chapters 4 through 9 constitute
Florence Davidson's first-person
account of her long and rich life.
The ornament that introduces her
narrative is a dogfish shark by her
grandson Robert Davidson.